Franklin's
Political Theories

Franklin's Political Theories

BY

MALCOLM R. EISELEN

1928

DOUBLEDAY, DORAN & COMPANY, INC.

Garden City, New York

COPYRIGHT, 1928, BY DOUBLEDAY, DORAN
& COMPANY, INC. ALL RIGHTS RESERVED.
PRINTED IN THE UNITED STATES AT THE
COUNTRY LIFE PRESS, GARDEN CITY, N. Y.
— C —
FIRST EDITION

Contents

Franklin's
Political Theories

Chapter I

FRANKLIN AS A POLITICAL THEORIST

IT IS not easy to trace the political theories of Benjamin Franklin. Unlike his contemporaries, John Adams and Thomas Jefferson, he has left no carefully reasoned scheme of political philosophy to interpret and to justify the events of which he was a part. His well-known aversion for the merely abstract, together with a multiplicity of more pressing duties, left neither time nor inclination to write an extended treatise upon the science of government. Instead, his ideas must be sought for, scattered through his writings, or, as is often the case, must be inferred as the unspoken motive for a given line of action.

The attempt to interpret Franklin's political ideas meets with another difficulty which is even more formidable. The creator of Poor Richard was an eminently practical man, whose political life was devoted to the attainment of certain highly practical ends. Thus it was that Franklin, the public servant, sometimes in the line of duty gave voice to sentiments which Franklin, the private individual, repudiated. All of his public, and much of his private political writings were intended to subserve a definite utilitarian purpose, and must be interpreted with due regard for their polemical origin. Even where his expressions were apparently sincere, they were subject to sudden change, as Franklin grew and learned by the light of experience, a healthy process which continued to the day of his death. The inevitable result was that Franklin's political theories were distinctly evolutionary in nature, shifting not so much in response to abstract philosophical reasoning as in relatively pliant submission to the exigencies of the times. Perhaps better than any other of the American leaders, he reflected the changing aspects of American public opinion throughout the entire course of the revolutionary period.

In justice to Franklin, it should be said that while his opinions might be swayed by considerations of public expediency, they were unmoved by arguments of private interest. During the Stamp Act controversy, fame and fortune were promised him if he would betray the colonial cause, but he could not be induced to yield a single step. It was no mere idle boast when he declared, "I thought it should not be expected of me to change my political Opinions every time his Majesty thought fit to change his Ministers. . . . My rule, in which I have always found satisfaction, is never to turn aside in public affairs through views of private interest; but to go straight forward in doing what appears to me right at the time, leaving the consequences with Providence." [1]

In a public cause, however, Franklin did not hesitate to shift his forces to a more tenable position, and the evidences of his political generalship are clearly

[1] Franklin (Smyth), V, 290.

to be seen in his writings. The readiness with which Franklin abandoned the old belief for the new frequently lays him open to the charge of inconsistency. Perhaps in this very fact lies the key to his success as a leader in a movement so consistently inconsistent as the American Revolution. Obviously pursuing what he regards as political expediency, he frequently slips into self-contradiction. Such inconsistencies cannot but add tremendously to the task of discovering just what were the fundamental tenets of Franklin's political belief. In such a study, care must be taken not to mistake expressions of expediency for those of conviction, or to confound the exception to the rule with the rule itself. Only by recognizing his distinct limitations as a political theorist and making due allowance for them can some degree of system be found in what often appears to be but confused and contradictory expressions of political thought.

Chapter II

THE SOURCES OF FRANKLIN'S THEORIES

AMERICAN political thought of the eighteenth century, in-so-far as it was influenced by particular writers, was derived from the pages of Milton, Sydney, Harrington, and Locke. The latter's *Two Treatises of Government*, in particular, had been absorbed by Americans as a sort of political gospel, which furnished a reasoned foundation for the very type of government which they desired.[1] Montesquieu and Rousseau were known to the colonists, but except where they reflected the precepts of the English school seemed to have comparatively little effect upon American thought.[2] Hobbes, of course, represented the well-nigh perfect antithesis of everything an American patriot should believe.

As a man of wide reading, Franklin was undoubtedly under the same general influences as his fellow countrymen. Occasional references in his writings indicate that he was familiar with the works of Milton,[3] Sydney,[4] Locke,[5] Montesquieu,[6] and Rousseau.[7] His writings, however, show no evidence of a

---

[1] Merriam, *A History of American Political Theories*, p. 89.
[2] Ibid., 91-92.
[3] Franklin (Smyth), VIII, 446.
[4] Franklin (Smyth), II, 391.
[5] Franklin (Smyth), I, 243; II, 387n; III, 28.
[6] Franklin (Smyth), IX, 295; *London Chronicle*, V, 594.
[7] Ibid., 334.

4

slavish enthusiasm for the philosophy of any one of these leaders of political thought. In a consideration of sources it is necessary to guard against a dangerous tendency to read a cause and effect relationship into what is mere parallelism. An original and inquisitive mind, such as Franklin's undeniably was, is likely to attach more weight to the teachings of its own experience and reasoning than to the precepts of others. It is altogether fair to say that his ideas sprang less from the long traditions of speculative philosophy than from the practical conditions of life and administration in the colonies. He should be pictured, therefore, as gleaning from many sources, but never hesitating to reject or modify the ideas of others, if they did not fit into his conception of the existing state.

Most of Franklin's political ideas may be found in the writings of Locke and Milton, with which, as has been said, he was perfectly familiar.[1] In fact, no signer of the American Declaration of Independence could afford to ignore these spokesmen of a former rebellion against royal prerogative. Locke's conception of the nature of government, with its corollaries of popular sovereignty and the right of revolution, was eagerly seized by Franklin as providing a timely philosophical basis for the practical politics of his day.[2] With Milton, too, he had much in common in his advocacy of religious toleration, unrestricted freedom of speech, and the assurance to the individual of

[1] Especially Locke's *Two Treatises of Government* and Milton's *Areopagitica* and *Tenure of Kings and Magistrates.*
[2] Cf. Chapter III, infra.

a wide sphere of action unrestrained by governmental regulation. Consciously or unconsciously, Franklin undoubtedly absorbed much from the works of these two authors.

In like manner, Franklin sometimes laid hold of a contemporary writer and made the latter's ideas his own. He had abundant opportunity to do this; for during the latter years of his life, few important political or economic works appeared which were not sent with the authors' compliments for the eminent philosopher's inspection.[1] Thus many of Franklin's ideas may be traced to the school of French Physiocrats, whose economic belief antedated and influenced Adam Smith's *Wealth of Nations*. From the time of his first visit to France in 1767 until his death, Franklin enjoyed the most friendly personal relations with the leaders of this movement. Their influence upon the more economic phases of his political theory will be discussed more at length in the proper place.[2]

The purpose of this brief summary has been to show how varied were the sources from which Franklin's political belief was drawn. Wherever possible, in the more detailed discussion which follows, an effort will be made to indicate the probable source of his particular ideas, as well as to orient them in relation to the thought of the time. It must not be for-

---

[1] Out of the 4,276 books in Franklin's library at the time of his death, the titles of about 1,350 are known. Many of these books are upon political subjects. See G. S. Eddy: *Dr. Benjamin Franklin's Library*, in *Proc. of the American Antiquarian Society*, XXXIV, 206-226. Over 800 pamphlets from Franklin's library are now in the Pennsylvania Historical Society at Philadelphia.

[2] Cf. Chapter X, infra.

gotten, however, that had all these sources been closed to him, it is not probable that Franklin's political theories would have been greatly altered. His ideas were essentially the product of his environment, and nothing which could not pass the rigid test of practical utility could hope for a permanent place in Franklin's political system.

Chapter III

MOST political philosophers are not content until they have established an elaborate philosophical conception of the basis of all human government. Franklin was satisfied, rather, to accept the political state as an existent entity, concerning the origin of which the practical mind had little need to trouble itself. Occasionally, however, he found in the nature of the state such arguments as might be applied to some impending problem of practical politics, and from his expressions at these times it is possible to reconstruct his ideas as to the fundamental nature of government.

From relatively infrequent references, it is evident that Franklin accepted the social compact theory of Locke and his followers. Like them, he had the conception of an original, pre-political state of nature in which men were absolutely free and equal—a condition which he thought admirably illustrated among the American Indians. This was not, as Hobbes believed, a state of "bellum omnium contra omnes," but rather a sort of armed neutrality, in which "the Savage's Bow, his Hatchet, and his Coat of Skins were sufficiently secured, without Law, by the fear of personal Resentment and Retaliation."[1] As the

[1] Franklin (Smyth), IX, 293.

8

wants and possessions of the individual increased, man conceived the necessity of some more ordered system of human relationships. Accordingly, government was created by means of a contract in which each one voluntarily surrendered enough of his absolute freedom to permit the establishment of an organized authority. This government was established "for the Security of our Liberties, Property, Religion and everything that is dear to us," [1] and was to be "nothing else but the Attendance of the Trustees of the People upon the Interest and Affairs of the People." [2] Since government had for its sole purpose the happiness and security of the individual, it closely followed that it could derive its just powers only from the consent of the governed.

According to Franklin, the social contract was a compact between equals, uniting for a common purpose.[3] He absolutely rejected Hobbes' proposition that submission to force represented an implied contractual relationship.[4] This acceptance of the principle of inherent equality accounts for the essentially democratic features of Franklin's political philosophy.[5] At the same time, within the limits prescribed by the implied contract, he believed that the power of the public will must be unrestricted. For instance, Franklin wrote concerning the duty of the citizen to pay taxes, "All the Property that is necessary to a

[1] Unpublished manuscript in library of Amer. Phil. Soc., Philadelphia.
[2] Franklin (Smyth), II, 26.
[3] Franklin's marginal note on Ramsay, *Thoughts on the Origin and Nature of Government*, pp. 10, 12.
[4] Cf. Hobbes, *Leviathan*, chap. 20.
[5] Cf. Chapter XII, infra.

Man, for the Conservation of the Individual and the Propagation of the Species, is his Natural Right, which none can justly deprive him of: But all Property superfluous to such purposes is the Property of the Publick, who, by their Laws, have created it, and who may therefore by other Laws dispose of it, whenever the Welfare of the Public shall demand such Disposition. He that does not like Civil Society on these Terms, let him retire and live among Savages." [1] It should be noted, however, that although Franklin thus subordinated the will of the individual to the welfare of the social organism, he believed in actual practice that it was expedient to leave the individual with as large a degree of freedom from governmental control as was possible.

Franklin's broad conception of the powers of government did not prevent him from affirming that there were things which it could not do. Like most of the colonists, he maintained the existence of a body of natural rights, antedating the existence of government and superior to it in authority.[2] Issuing from these human rights and reinforcing them, were those fundamental rights of all Englishmen which found expression in the imperishable provisions of the Magna Charta, the Petition of Right, and the Bill of Rights. Taken collectively, these rights constitute the essence of the cherished institution of civil liberty, "that heavenly Blessing, without which Mankind lose

[1] Franklin (Smyth), IX, 138. Cf. Locke, *Two Treatises of Government*, II, sect. 96.
[2] Cf. Locke, *Two Treatises of Government*, II, sec. 135-142.

half their Dignity and Value." [1] The existence of
these rights was so self-evident to Franklin that he
mentions them only incidentally, but among those
which he specifically enumerates are the familiar
triumvirate of life, liberty, and property; freedom of
speech and religion; the right of petition, and the
right of unrestricted migration. Of these, the most
vital to all eighteenth-century Americans was the
right to the enjoyment of property; for around that
principle the entire revolutionary controversy came
to be centered. On this point, Franklin consistently
maintained the popular view. "Do not every Man's
Feelings," he said, "declare that his Property is not to
be taken from him without his consent?" [2]

From these great underlying principles, Franklin
followed Locke in the easy transition to the acceptance of the indefeasible right of revolution.[3] Since
the people were to be considered the basis of all
legitimate political authority, no sovereignty could
come into existence or continue to exist unless the
people consented to and authorized it. Where a
government became destructive of the very ends for
which it was established, it was the natural right and
duty of the people to change it.[4] Although Franklin
labored to the last to preserve the unity of the British
empire, he never denied that the colonies had a moral
and legal right to separate, whenever the imperial

1 Unpublished manuscript in library of Amer. Phil. Soc., Philadelphia.
2 Franklin's note on Ramsay, op. cit., p. 27.
3 Cf. Locke, *Two Treatises of Government*, II, sec. 149, 221-222.
4 Unpublished manuscript in library of University of Pennsylvania, Philadelphia, Pa.

connection failed to justify its continued existence.

These briefly, were the fundamental principles of Franklin's political creed. They were neither original nor unique, but were shared by most Americans of the time. Such widely divergent beliefs as those of Thomas Jefferson and Alexander Hamilton were reared upon exactly the same foundations. The distinguishing features of his theory must be sought in the refinements of detail with which these principles were applied. Strictly utilitarian in nature, Franklin's political theories cannot be divorced from their settings, but rather must be considered in close relation to the events which produced them. For this reason, the detailed discussion which follows is episodic rather than topical, and has been, wherever possible, centered about outstanding events in Franklin's political career.

Chapter IV

FRANKLIN AND THE ALBANY PLAN

Until about the year 1754, Franklin seems to have given scant thought to the science of government. During these early years, his attention was centered upon his printing business, his scientific experiments, and the internal improvement of his city and province. In his many public-spirited and philanthropic activities of this period, Franklin first manifested that passion for coöperative effort in a common cause, which, when applied to a broader field, was to form the fundamental basis of his political creed. The transcendent impulse of Franklin's political life was the belief that in mutual helpfulness and coöperation lay the one great hope of human progress. The ultimate ideal which he kept ever before him was the union of all the nations of the world in the interests of universal peace. He was not a man, however, to scorn the day of small beginnings, and in the pressing need for a closer colonial union he found close at hand an opportunity to apply, on a limited but none-the-less important scale, this dominating principle.

The Albany Congress of 1754 had been called by the Lords of Trade for the primary purpose of conciliating the Six Nations by renewing a treaty which would prevent them from going over to the French in the conflict which was impending. The Congress assembled on June 19, 1754, with representatives present from seven colonies. Franklin was one of the commissioners from Pennsylvania. With hostilities already broken out on the western frontier, the delegates soon saw that an agreement with the Indians must be supplemented by some plan of concerted action among the colonies themselves. On June 24, it was unanimously resolved that a union of all the colonies was "absolutely necessary for their security and defence," and Franklin was made a member of the committee which was appointed "to prepare and receive plans or schemes for the union of the colonies, and to digest them into one general plan." [1]

Franklin, with characteristic foresight, had already sketched the outline of such a plan, which he had submitted to several of his friends for suggestions. When the members of the committee met, several plans were presented, but Franklin's was the basis of the one reported to the convention. After twelve days of spirited debate, the Plan of Union was adopted, on July 10, and was submitted to the provinces for ratification. If approved by the latter, the plan was to be sent to England to be established by act of Parliament. The colonies, however, without exception refused to ratify it, on the grounds that it gave too much power to the Crown; so that the project never actually came before the home government. [2]

[1] The official minutes of the Congress are in the *Doc. Rel. to the Col. Hist. of N. Y.*, VI, 853-892.

[2] Franklin's often-quoted statement that "the Crown disapproved it, as having placed too much Weight in the Democratic Part of the Constitution" (Franklin (Smyth), III, 227n.), is therefore not strictly correct.

Briefly, the Albany Plan provided for a President-General, appointed and maintained by the Crown, and a Grand Council, chosen by the Assemblies of the different colonies. The colonies were to be represented upon the Council in proportion to their contributions to the common treasury. Elections were to be held triennially. The business to be intrusted to this body included the management of all matters relating to the Indians, to military and naval affairs, and to the establishment of western settlements. For these purposes, power was given to make laws and to levy such duties and taxes as would distribute an equal burden throughout the colonies. The acts of the Grand Council were made subject to the veto of the President-General and of the King in Council. The entire executive power was to be vested in the President-General, perhaps assisted by an executive council of the colonial governors.[1]

The general conception of such a plan was by no means original with Franklin. For over a century the French and Indian menace had made tragically clear the necessity for some form of defensive union among the English colonies. The first movement in this direction was the New England Confederation of 1643, from which Franklin unquestionably derived many of the features of his proposed government.[2] Further gropings toward an effectual system of inter-colonial coöperation are shown after 1684 in the successive conferences which took place, chiefly for the con-

[1] The text of the Albany Plan is in Franklin (Smyth), III, 226 ff.
[2] *American Political Science Review*, VIII, 393-412.

sideration of Indian affairs. In 1697, William Penn proposed a Congress of delegates from all the colonies to adjust matters of difference between the various provinces and to provide for the common defence.[1] The following year, Charles Davenant, an English writer, commended Penn's plan of union and urged the formation of a "national assembly" for the consideration of all matters relative to the general welfare. According to both of these proposals, each colony was to have an equal vote. In 1701, an anonymous Virginian first advanced a plan of union based upon proportional representation—a principle adopted by Franklin in his Albany plan. In the same year, Robert Livingston suggested a consolidation into three regional unions,[2] a system which Franklin specifically rejected, as offering only a partial solution to the problem.[3] Other plans were proposed from time to time by the Lords of Trade or by crown officials, but these were obviously designed to exalt the functions of the royal governors at the expense of popular rights and privileges, and accordingly carried slight weight with the author of the Albany Plan.

One of the most significant of the early plans of union was presented by Daniel Coxe in 1722.[4] In all probability, Franklin used this proposal as the starting point for his own draft. Both plans provide for a Governor-General appointed by the Crown and a congress of delegates chosen by the popular assemblies.

[1] *Doc. Rel. to the Col. Hist. of N. Y.*, IV, 297.
[2] Ibid., 874.
[3] Franklin (Smyth), III, 205.
[4] Coxe, *A Description of the English Province of Carolana*, Preface.

By each the Governor-General was given a veto, and the Grand Council, with his consent, was to determine the quotas of men, money, and provisions the colonies should contribute to the common defence. The general structure of each plan is essentially that of a Crown Colony applied to the broader field of a colonial federation. Franklin's plan, however, is by far the more detailed. In 1752, Archibald Kennedy published a scheme of union which, like Franklin's, stressed the utility of colonial coöperation in western land development.[1] This plan was submitted to Franklin before publication, and was printed with a letter expressing his heartiest commendation of the project, although he believed that any movement for union must come through the people rather than through the colonial governors.[2] In the same year, Governor Dinwiddie, of Virginia, recommended the merging of the provinces into two great political divisions, north and south. The Plan of Union proposed in 1754 by the Lords of Trade came too late to influence Franklin's plan and was at most a union for military purposes, not a political federation.[3]

Franklin was undoubtedly familiar with most, if not all, of these proposals for the political unification of British America.[4] The Albany plan is significant, therefore, because of its selective features rather than as an original contribution. This fact, however,

---

[1] Kennedy, *The Importance of Gaining and Preserving the Friendship of the Indians to the British Interest Considered.*
[2] Franklin (Smyth), III, 40.
[3] *Doc. Rel. to the Col. Hist. of N. Y.*, VI, 903-906.
[4] For a convenient compilation of the various plans of union of the colonial period see Carson, *The Const. of the U. S.*, II, 439-503.

makes it no less valuable as an indication of Franklin's political theories at this time.

Franklin did not wholly approve of the Albany Plan in the form in which it was adopted by the Congress, although he heartily favored its acceptance as a step in the right direction. There were, he wrote, "some Improvements that I think necessary but could not get inserted in the Plan." [1] This is not to be wondered at in what was so frankly a compromise measure, framed in the vain hope that it would find favor on both sides of the Atlantic. In general, however, it is safe to say that he agreed with its provisions. From the standpoint of imperial theory, the Plan recognized the subordinate position of the proposed colonial union by providing for the disallowance by the King in Council of the acts of the colonial Grand Council. Not until the actual outbreak of the Revolution would Franklin have denied this right to his sovereign. [2] He would, however, have preferred a plan of union voluntarily entered into by the colonies themselves, rather than one imposed by act of Parliament, because the former would "be more easy to alter and improve, as Circumstances should require and Experience direct." [3] He also would probably have preferred not to lodge the support of the President-General in the Crown, but such a provision was absolutely essential if ratification by the home government was to be expected. At the same time, he steadfastly insisted that the Grand Council be elected

[1] Letters of Cadwallader Colden, IV, 458.
[2] Cf. Chapters VI, VII, infra.
[3] Franklin (Smyth), III, 42.

solely by the representatives of the people. No other
arrangement was possible if the plan was to safeguard
the "undoubted right of Englishmen, not to be taxed
but by their own consent given through their representatives." [1] Thus, in 1754, Franklin sounded the
battle cry of the Revolution, but it is certain that
neither he nor any of his colleagues realized the tremendous forces which lay dormant in this apparently
innocent declaration of faith.

Coxe's plan of 1722 had provided for the equal
representation of the colonies in the General Council.
Franklin, however, substituted the more democratic
provision of proportional representation based on
contributions to the common support. The provision
for triennial elections is of interest in contrast to the
quite general American feeling that "where annual
elections end, there slavery begins." [2] If this particular article had Franklin's support, it is indicative
of a greater trust in representative government than
was common at the time. The moderate provision
which the Plan makes for the salaries of Council members is unquestionably an application of Franklin's
favorite idea that a public office should be held for
service and not for gain. It is not likely, however,
that the plan represents Franklin's ideal of a cen-
tralized government. The necessity of placating
inter-colonial jealousy, doubtless, made it impossible
for him to give free rein to the strong national im-
pulses which he manifested elsewhere. It is altogether
probable that some of the "improvements" which

1 Franklin (Smyth), III, 233.
2 John Adams, *Works*, IV, 205.

were rejected by the Congress were in the direction of greater power for the general government.

Despite its unceremonious rejection, Franklin, to the end of his life, retained faith in his Plan of Union. In his *Autobiography* he wrote, "I am still of opinion that it would have been happy for both sides the water if it had been adopted. The colonies, so united, would have been sufficiently strong to have defended themselves; there would then have been no need of troops from England; of course, the subsequent pretence for taxing America, and the bloody contest it occasioned, would have been avoided." [1]   It is of interest to note that as late as 1788, when this was written, the old man still regretted the necessity which had left to the English colonies no alternative save absolute and irretrievable separation.

[1] Franklin (Smyth), I, 388.

Chapter V

FRANKLIN AND PROPRIETARY GOVERNMENT

CLOSE upon the Albany Congress came the formal
outbreak of the Seven Years' War. The British dis-
asters of the opening years of that conflict quickly
precipitated a crisis in the internal affairs of Pennsylvania. There the proprietors had consistently refused
to submit to the taxation of their immense estates.
The result was a never-ending conflict between the
popular assembly and the proprietary governor, who
was under bond to obey the instructions of the owners.
While roving bands of savages ravaged English settlements within sixty miles of Philadelphia,[1] the contest-
ing parties stubbornly refused to vote military
supplies except upon their own terms. In the face
of such pressing need for extraordinary measures of
defence, the controversy soon took on a tragic significance. As a last resort, the Pennsylvania Assembly
sent Franklin as its agent to London to secure a modi-
fication of the proprietary instructions relative to
taxation.

Ever since his first election to the Assembly in 1752,
Franklin had been one of the leaders of the anti-pro-
prietary party. Parkman charges that in this controversy he was animated solely by the selfish motives

[1] Parkman, *Montcalm and Wolfe*, I, 347.

of partizan politics, which completely blinded him to the larger interests of the public good.[1]   Such a criticism, however, implies a narrowness of vision and a disregard for human suffering wholly uncharacteristic of Franklin.   There is evidence, rather, that he felt the situation keenly; for to this period of almost complete cessation of the functions of government may be attributed Franklin's never-ending hostility to a bicameral legislature, or any other device tending to retard the wheels of government.   Had agreement been possible, it is probable that this great master of the art of compromise would have been the first to seek it.

Franklin's uncompromising attitude may be best explained by reference to his political expressions of the period.   He believed that the situation was the inevitable result of a defective form of government, and was not to be remedied by any temporary makeshift.   Such a system of feudal proprietorship was thoroughly repugnant to a man of Franklin's democratic tendencies.   From London he wrote, "I believe it will in time be clearly seen by all thinking People that the Government and Property of a Province should not be in the same Family."[2]   He sought to divest the controversy of all personalities by declaring, "Disputes . . . have arisen in All Proprietary

[1] Parkman, *Montcalm and Wolfe*, I, 349.   Parkman is one of the few American writers who attempt to justify the proprietary position.

[2] Franklin (Smyth), III, 472.   Contrast this with Harrington's theory that supreme authority should rest with those who own most of the property in the community.   (*Oceana*, 1747 ed., p. 39.)   It is said that William Penn found in the *Oceana* the inspiration for many of the features of the Pennsylvania constitution.   (Russell Smith, *Harrington and his Oceana*, pp. 169-179.)

Governments and subsisted till their Dissolution . . .
I see no Reason to suppose that all Proprietary Rulers
are worse Men than other Rulers, nor that all People
in Proprietary Governments are worse People than
those in other Governments. I suspect therefore,
that the Cause is radical, interwoven in the Constitution, and so become of the very Nature of Proprietary
Governments."¹ The only solution which he believed to be at once practical and efficacious was "an
immediate Royal Government, without the Interven-
tion of Proprietary Powers."²

In June, 1760, after three years of litigation,
Franklin brought to a close the immediate controversy
with the proprietors, who at last recognized the right
of taxing the proprietary estates. It soon became evident, however, that he was right in attributing the
trouble to the inherent defects of the system. Internal disturbances increased with a rapidity which
the proprietary governor was either unwilling or unable to check. After a bitter factional fight, Franklin was again sent to England, in November, 1764,
this time bearing a petition to the King from the
Assembly of Pennsylvania requesting a change from
proprietary to royal government. The petition,
drafted by Franklin himself, recited the various evils
arising from proprietary government and assured his
Majesty that they were not likely "to receive any
Remedy here, the continual Disputes between the
Proprietaries and People, and their mutual Jealousies

¹ Franklin (Smyth), IV, 227-228.
² Ibid., 231.

and Dislikes preventing." [1]   The excitement attend-
ing the passage of the Stamp Act and subsequent
events prevented any serious consideration of the petition by the home government.   Franklin was left,
therefore, free to take a leading part as the spokesman of America in the greatest constitutional crisis
the British Empire has ever known.   It was a controversy waged chiefly in the realm of political
theory, and provides an interesting study of how
Franklin's theories at the same time influenced and
were influenced by the course of events around him.

[1] Franklin (Smyth), IV, 314.

Chapter VI

FRANKLIN'S THEORY OF THE BRITISH EMPIRE

PRIOR to 1764, Americans gave little thought to the political theory of the British Empire. Except for the mild restraints of the Navigation Acts and, occasionally, an offensive royal governor, the colonists were well satisfied with existing conditions. The Declaratory Resolves of 1764 and the resultant Stamp Act of 1765 burst upon them, therefore, in the light of cruel and unusual innovations, which put existing imperial relations in a startlingly new light. The history of American political thought of the succeeding decade is an attempt to justify philosophically the not unnatural opposition to the theory—so dramatically reasserted—of the Parliamentary right of complete legislative authority over his Majesty's American dominions. The task was not easy; for the Parliamentary position was sustained both by precedent and by the opinion of the ablest jurists of the time, and had been formerly accepted even among the colonists themselves.[1]

[1] It was probably true, as a British pamphleteer said, that there were "almost as many instances of Parliament's exercising supreme legislative jurisdiction over the colonies, as there have been sessions of Parliament since the first settlement of America." (Knox, *The Claim of the Colonies to an Exemption from Internal Taxes imposed by the Authority of Parliament Examined*, p. 9.) Even so advanced a revolutionist as James Otis declared in 1765 that "the Parliament have the same right to levy internal taxes on the colonies as to regulate trade; and the right of levying both is undoubtedly in Parliament." (Otis, *A Vindication of the British Colonies*, pp. 29, 30.)

the colonies were not represented, Franklin's early expressions are not altogether consistent. At the time of the Albany Congress, a project for colonial taxation by act of Parliament was seriously considered in England and seems to have been suggested to Franklin by Governor Shirley.[1] Franklin replied that "to pay immediate heavy taxes, in the laying . . . of which we have no part . . . must seem hard measure to Englishmen, who cannot conceive, that by hazarding their lives and fortunes, in subduing and settling new countries, extending the dominion, and increasing the commerce of the mother nation, they have forfeited the native rights of Britons." [2] The entire Revolutionary period nowhere offers a more explicit expression of the rights of Englishmen than this, written by Franklin in 1754.

In marked contrast were Franklin's expressions concerning the Stamp Act when that measure was first passed. Nowhere did he intimate that he regarded the Act as exceeding the constitutional jurisdiction of Parliament. As an inexpedient and burdensome measure, he earnestly opposed it, but once passed, the only advice he could give his countrymen was to submit to it in a spirit of "firm Loyalty to the Crown & faithful Adherence to the Government of this Nation." [3] With characteristic prudence, he sent his printing partner, David Hall, one hundred reams of "large Half Sheets," by using which

---

[1] Shirley believed that such a tax was both desirable and constitutional. (*Correspondence of William Shirley*, I, 479.)

[2] Franklin (Smyth), III, 236.

[3] Franklin (Smyth), IV, 392.

he might lighten the burden of the impending tax,[1] and even recommended one of his friends and neighbors for the office of local stamp agent.[2]   Such an attitude of patient submission to the inevitable was assuredly not that of a man who felt himself despoiled of the fundamental rights of an Englishman, particularly of a man who, as he later declared, would "freely spend nineteen shillings in the pound to defend the right of giving or refusing the other shilling." [3]

It is utterly impossible to reconcile Franklin's attitude at this time with his previous and later expressions upon the subject.   His words would seem to indicate either that at this time he accepted as valid the theory of Parliamentary supremacy, or that he was willing to sacrifice his rights and those of his countrymen upon the alter of imperial harmony. The latter hypothesis is perhaps the more probable, and offers a striking example of the degree to which Franklin could subordinate mere theory to the practical needs of the moment.   Whatever may have been the motivating impulse, it is certain that for once in his life, Franklin was strangely out of touch with the public sentiment of America.   Once informed of that, he immediately provided a political doctrine to justify it.   If Franklin's imperial theory at times resembled the chameleon, it was at least not wanting in resourcefulness.

[1] Franklin (Smyth), IV, 363.   [3] Franklin (Bigelow), III, 485.
[2] Franklin (Smyth), VI, 201.

The theory adopted by Franklin at this time was based upon the somewhat tenuous distinction between internal and external taxes.   He admitted the general right of Parliament to legislate for the colonies and to levy customs duties (external taxes) for the regulation of commerce, but denied to it the right to levy excise taxes (internal taxes) upon the colonists. The distinction, as made in his famous Examination before the House of Commons,[1] was this, "An external tax is a duty laid on commodities imported; that duty is added to the first cost and other charges on the commodity, and, when it is offered to sale, makes a part of the price.   If the people do not like it at that price, they refuse it; they are not obliged to pay it.   But an internal tax is forced from the people without their consent, if not laid by their own representatives.   The stamp act says, we shall have no commerce, make no exchange of property with each other, neither purchase, nor grant, nor recover debts; we shall neither marry nor make our wills, unless we pay such and such sums; and thus it is intended to extort our money from us, or ruin us by the consequences of refusing to pay it." [2]   When asked what would happen if Parliament should lay a duty upon some imported article necessary to the life of the colonists, he merely denied the existence of any such commodity.   Thus, by a clever evasion, he avoided an admission which would have been all but fatal to

[1] February, 1766.
[2] For complete Examination, see Franklin (Smyth), IV, 413-448.

the distinction he wished to establish.   In this examination, Franklin also repeatedly affirmed the natural right of Englishmen not to be taxed without their common consent.   He denied the proposition that the colonists were "virtually" represented in Parliament, and declared that if all that one has can be taken away by laws passed by a distant legislature in which one has no voice, then there is the end of natural right and the beginning of slavery.   He warned the members that no force would ever compel the colonists to accept so unjust a measure, and that attempts at coercion would only result in useless bloodshed.   On the subject of his personal attitude, Franklin replied, "I have a great many debts due me in America, and I had rather they should remain unrecoverable by any law, than submit to the Stamp Act," a sentiment decidedly in advance of the submissive attitude which he had displayed earlier.

In maintaining a distinction between internal and external taxation, Franklin was not without distinguished support.   William Pitt expressed the same sentiment when he declared, "The Commons of America, represented in their several Assemblies, have ever been in possession of the exercise of this, their constitutional right, of giving and granting their own money.   They would have been slaves if they had not enjoyed it.   At the same time, this kingdom, as the supreme governing and legislative body, has always bound the colonies by her laws, by her regulations and restrictions in trade, in navigation, in manufactures,

in everything, except that of taking their money out
of their pockets without their consent." [1]   In America, the moderate resolutions of the Stamp Act Congress, while claiming for the colonists the inherent
right of Englishmen not to be taxed without their
own consent, at the same time freely acknowledged
their "due subordination to that august body, the
parliament of Great Britain." [2]   In recognizing the
supremacy and primacy of the English Parliament in
all fields save that of internal taxation, these resolutions contained nothing which might not, at this
time, have been written by Franklin himself.

Unfortunately, even then this attractive doctrine
was seen to be untenable. So distinguished a jurist
as Lord Mansfield declared, "I know no difference
between laying internal and external taxes," [3] and
Charles Townshend thought the distinction between
internal and external taxes "perfect nonsense." [4] The
authority of sovereignty is essentially absolute and in-
divisible. A tax is a tax, whether indirect or direct,
and if, as Pitt said, Parliament had no constitutional
power to "take money out of their pockets" without
their consent, one method was as unconstitutional as
the other.

The colonists were not long in discovering that this
theory was not only false, but contained an admission
distinctly dangerous to their cause. Taking Franklin
at his word, Parliament repealed the obnoxious Stamp

[1] Hansard, *Parliamentary History*, XVI, 100.
[2] Niles, *Principles and Acts of the Revolution*, p. 457.
[3] Hansard, *Parliamentary History*, XVI, 176.
[4] *Collections of the Massachusetts Historical Society*, 5th Series, Vol. IX, 215.

Act, and replaced it with a system of supposedly allowable import duties. The fallacy of their former theory was thus forcibly brought home to American political thinkers, who suddenly found it necessary to discover a new philosophical formula for securing freedom from Parliamentary taxation, while maintaining America's loyal participation in the British Empire. In this second stage in the evolution of American imperial theory, John Dickinson stands out as the spokesman of the colonies.

Dickinson's arguments were developed in his *Letters from a Farmer in Pennsylvania,* which were first published in 1767. He conceded the right of Parliament to regulate the trade of the Empire, and hence exercise a legislative authority over the colonies, but denied to that body the right to levy taxes of any kind whatever.[1] He admitted that this regulation might take the form of duties, but made a distinction between duties primarily for revenue and those for the regulation of trade. Into which category a given impost fell was to be determined solely by the "intention" of the framers of the law. Thus, with delightful naïveté, he substituted for the arbitrary distinction of Franklin, an even more arbitrary distinction of his own.

Dickinson's reasoning was undoubtedly instrumental in forcing Franklin to abandon his distinction between the kinds of taxes which Parliament could or could not impose. As late as April, 1767, he still held, at least in his public utterances, to the doctrine

---

[1] Dickinson, *Letters from a Farmer in Pennsylvania,* pp. 7, 14.

whole Empire, allowed I mean by the Farmer, though
I think whoever would dispute that right might stand
upon firmer ground, and make much more of the
argument." [1]

If at times the sentiments here expressed seem confused and contradictory, they probably merely reflected the uncertainty in the mind of the writer.
Under the force of circumstance and the exigencies
of argument, Franklin was groping toward a doctrine
which was beginning vaguely to be felt by many
Americans. In 1766, Robert Bland had advanced the
opinion that "though a part of the British Empire,
America was no part of the kingdom of England,"
and that, having been "settled by Englishmen at their
own expense, under particular stipulations with the
Crown," it was under no obligation to receive laws
from Parliament.[2] As early as 1765, Governor Hop-
kins of Rhode Island had declared the Britannic
dominions to constitute an "Imperial State" consisting of "many separate governments, in which no
single part, though greater than any other part, is by
that superiority entitled to make laws for, or to tax
such lesser part." [3] Although neither of these works
are specifically mentioned by Franklin, a close verbal
similarity in some of his writing would make it seem
not unlikely that he had both read and been influenced by their doctrines. Such a prodigious innovation in constitutional theory was not to be

[1] Franklin (Smyth), V, 114-116.
[2] Bland, *An Enquiry into the Rights of the British Colonies*, pp. 20, 24.
[3] *Rhode Island Records*, VI, 424.

adopted lightly, but once having taken the decisive step of denying to Parliament all right to legislate for the American colonies, Franklin never retreated. He believed that the British Parliament had no authority but within the realm, and that the American colonies were manifestly not within the realm.[1] The logical conclusion was that "the Parliament of Great Britain has not, never had, and of right never can have, without consent given either before or after, power to make laws of sufficient force to bind the subjects in America in any case whatever, and particularly in taxation."[2] With this unequivocal assertion of his position, the question definitely assumed for him a place among those truths which were self-evident and needed no longer to be argued.

Franklin's new position in no way destroyed his conception of the unity and integrity of the British Empire. Soon after the above letter was written, he ceased to expect or even to deem desirable a union in Parliament,[3] but he believed the colonies bound as firmly as ever to the mother country in the person of the sovereign. "The British empire is not a single state; it comprehends many," he wrote. "We have the same King, but not the same legislatures."[4] The relation of the King to his colonies he defined as follows, "By our Constitution he is, with his plantation Parliaments, the sole Legislator of his American Sub-

[1] Franklin's note on Ramsay, op. cit., p. 50.
[2] Franklin (Bigelow), III, 485.
[3] Franklin (Bigelow), IV, 310.
[4] Franklin (Smyth), V, 280.

Chapter VII

FRANKLIN AND INDEPENDENCE

THROUGHOUT the long controversy which preceded the Revolution, Franklin never wavered in his steadfast devotion to the British Empire. As has been seen, his first instinct was to submit even to the exactions of the Stamp Act, rather than to risk the loss of so precious a heritage. Far from being opposed to monarchical government, he saw exemplified in Britain "the best constitution, and the best King, any nation was ever blessed with." [1] If Parliament was foolish, obstinate, and corrupt, that might easily be remedied, so far as the colonies were concerned, by denying to it all part in American affairs. It is no wonder, therefore, that he regarded a separation as an unmitigated misfortune, and repeatedly lamented the stupid indifference by which successive blundering ministries were making American independence inevitable. During a period when American public opinion was essentially conciliatory, no one labored more earnestly and unremittingly than Franklin to perpetuate a political union based upon the enduring principles of liberty and mutual confidence.

At the same time, it must be recognized that by

[1] Franklin (Smyth), V, 133. Cf. John Adams, who called the British constitution "the most stupendous fabric of human invention." (Adams, *Works,* IV, 358.)

1768 Franklin, in his imperial theory, had adopted a view which, when the time was ripe, might easily be turned into a justification of complete independence. His belief united an acceptance of the natural rights philosophy of government with a conception of the British Empire as a confederation of free peoples, voluntarily submitting themselves to the same king by a compact entered into, and terminable, at the will of the people concerned. Whatever may have been the sentiments of his heart, in his philosophical belief he was fully prepared for a declaration of independence.

It is difficult to say at what moment the possibility of separation first presented itself to Franklin. Dr. Benjamin Rush tells of a conversation with Franklin in 1785, in which the latter is quoted as saying that "the foundation of the American Revolution was laid in 1733, by a clause in a bill to subject the Colonies to being govern'd by Royal instructions, which was rejected. He said, in 1756 [1] when he went to England, he had a long conversation with Mr. Pratt (afterwards Lord Camden) who told him that Britain would drive the colonies to independence. This, he said, first led him to realize its occurring shortly." [2] Franklin's own earliest reference to possible independence occurs in a letter to Governor Shirley, dated December 22, 1754. In this letter, he strongly ad-

---

[1] This is a slight error. Franklin did not go to England until the following year. XXIX, 23.

[2] *Penn. Mag. of Hist.* Lord Camden was one of the few Englishmen who accepted the colonial view that an act of Parliament might be "illegal, contrary to the fundamental laws of nature, contrary to the fundamental laws of this constitution." (Hansard, *Parliamentary History*, XVI, 178.)

vocated colonial representation in Parliament, and, as
one of his arguments, declared that it would "greatly
lessen the danger of future separation." [1]   On the
other hand, in his Canada pamphlet of 1760, he pro-
nounced any concerted action for colonial independence as "not merely improbable, it is impossible." [2]
It should be remembered, however, that this paper
was expressly written as a work of propaganda for
the annexation of Canada, a project to which the possibility of colonial independence would have been absolutely fatal.   Franklin's fears of separation appear
for the first time to have taken definite shape at the
time of the Stamp Act.   He apprehended that the
colonists, through the "Madness of the Populace or
their blind Leaders" might resort to "Acts of a rebel-
lious tendency." [3]   In January, 1766, in a letter to the
London press, he warned the English people that any
attempt to collect taxes laid by Parliament would inevitably result in bloodshed. [4]   At the same time, he
seems to have believed that, with the principal cities
of America at the mercy of the English fleet, actual
secession was a military impossibility. [5]   With a self-
assurance which is characteristically American, he
believed that a maintenance of the union was more
essential to the happiness and prosperity of Britain
than of America, and hoped that British statesmen
would not be blind to their own interest. [6]   At the
same time he shrewdly suggested that to allow "each

[1] Franklin (Smyth), III, 239.
[2] Franklin (Smyth), IV, 71.
[3] Ibid., 392.
[4] Ibid., 403.
[5] Franklin (Bigelow), III, 469.
[6] Franklin (Smyth), V, 21.

colony to send Members to Parliament" would promote a mutual better understanding, and would "forever preserve the Union which otherwise may be
various Ways broken, as by Division in the Royal
Family." [1]   As tactless ministries and a haughty
Parliament constantly multiplied colonial dissatisfac-
tion, Franklin saw with regret the danger of separation becoming more acute.   In 1768, he wrote to his
son, "I apprehend a breach between the two countries." [2]   Three years later, he informed the Massachusetts Assembly that "one may clearly see, in the
system of customs to be exacted in America by act
of Parliament, the seeds sown of a total disunion of
the two countries, though, as yet, that event may be
at a considerable distance." [3]

With true human reverence for the explicit, it is
traditional to accept January 29, 1774, as the date
upon which Franklin was converted to the great
truth of American independence.   On that day, he
was brought before the privy council of England,
ostensibly upon public business, but in reality to stand
silent before that body while for sixty minutes the
infamous Wedderburn lashed him with the scourge of
malignant personal abuse.   As illustrative of the
criminal intolerance of British crown officials, the in-
cident is indeed significant, but as an alleged turning
point in Franklin's political thought, it has been much
over-emphasized.   It is true that on November 27,
1774, Josiah Quincy wrote from London, "His

[1] Unpublished manuscript in library of Am. Phil. Soc., Philadelphia.
[2] Franklin (Smyth), V, 148.
[3] Quincy, *Memoir of the Life of Josiah Quincy, Jr.*, p. 250.

(Franklin's) ideas are not contracted within the narrow limits of exemption from taxes, but are extended upon the broad scale of total emancipation."[1] This ambiguous statement might be interpreted to mean an acceptance of the principle of absolute independence, but in all probability refers merely to that complete independence of Parliament which Franklin had accepted years before. Certain it is that during the fourteen months that he still remained in England, he in no way abated his efforts to avert the rupture that was rapidly becoming inevitable. To this end, he pledged his entire personal fortune in compensation for the tea destroyed at Boston, stipulating only that the offensive acts of Parliament should be repealed,[2] and engaged in the last futile peace negotiations through Lord Howe and his sister.[3] During these negotiations, which extended from December, 1774, to February, 1775, Franklin, although insisting upon the full rights of the colonies, manifested an earnest desire for agreement. He wrote to Lord Howe that even then "tears of joy . . . wet my cheek" at the prospect of a possible reconciliation.[4] When, on March 21, 1775, Franklin sailed for America, he could say with a clear conscience that he had done his utmost to prevent the final break.

Not for a moment, however, was Franklin ready to sacrifice the fundamental rights of the American

[1] Franklin (Smyth), V, 317.
[2] Franklin (Smyth), VI, 394.
[3] For Franklin's own account of these negotiations, see Franklin (Smyth), VI, 318-399.
[4] Franklin (Smyth), VI, 461.

colonies. These essentials of human liberty must be maintained even at the cost of the beloved imperial connection. To what lengths he was prepared to go is shown by a private memorandum, which was written while he was still in England, and which is worthy to be quoted in full, as revealing an intensity of feeling not often found in the writings of the calm philosopher. Apostrophizing the English people, he writes,

"We know your Power can crush us:—but 'tis time enough to submit to absolute Power when we can no longer resist it, when those who chuse rather to die in Defense of their Liberty than consent to Slavery are accordingly dead: When those who chuse to spend all their Property in defending it, rather than give it up to the insolent groundless Claims of Oppressors, have spent it—This Nation looks upon us at present with perhaps too much Contempt. It is worth while to struggle bravely and run some Risque of Life and Fortune, were it only that we might prove ourselves worthy of the Race from whence we sprung and obtain some Share of your Esteem." [1]

It is characteristic, however, that these fiery sentiments, worthy of a Samuel Adams or a Patrick Henry, were not published to the world, but were locked closely in Franklin's heart, while he earnestly labored to avert the final catastrophe which they anticipated.

As late as the summer of 1775, Franklin was not

[1] Unpublished manuscript in the library of the Amer. Phil. Soc., Philadelphia.

yet ready to sever all connection with the mother country. On June 27, he wrote to John Sargent, a friendly member of Parliament, "It now requires great Wisdom on your Side the Water to prevent a total Separation; I hope it will be found among you. We shall give you one Opportunity more of recovering our Affections and retaining the Connection; and that I fear will be the last." [1] This letter marks the beginning of the end of Franklin's hopes for the maintenance of the imperial relation. Ten days later he wrote, "I think I am not half so reconcileable now, as I was a Month ago." [2] On July 21, he submitted his Articles of Confederation for the consideration of the Continental Congress.[3] The plan provided for a Union of the Colonies, which was to continue in effect "till the Terms of Reconciliation proposed in the Petition of the last Congress to the King are agreed to; till the Acts since made, restraining the American Commerce are repeal'd; till Reparation is made for the Injury done to Boston, by shutting up its Port, for the Burning of Charlestown, and for the Expence of this unjust War; and till all the British Troops are withdrawn from America. On the Arrival of these Events, the Colonies return to their former Connection and Friendship with Britain: But on Failure thereof, this Confederation is to be perpetual." [4] This qualified declaration of independence was Franklin's last offering upon the altar of conciliation. From that

[1] Franklin (Smyth), VI, 407.
[2] Unpublished manuscript in library of William S. Mason.
[3] Cf. Chapter VIII, infra.
[4] Franklin (Smyth), VI, 424.

time on, Franklin sorrowfully but resolutely took his place among the ever-increasing band of patriots who recognized that the parting of the ways had come. With quiet resignation, he wrote on April 26, 1777, "I long laboured in England, with great zeal and sincerity, to prevent the breach that has happened, and which is now so wide that no endeavors of mine can possibly heal it." [1]

On June 7, 1776, Richard Henry Lee rose in the Continental Congress and solemnly presented the resolution that "these united colonies are and of right ought to be free and independent States, that they are absolved from all allegiance to the British Crown, and that all political connection between them and the State of Great Britain is and ought to be totally dissolved." [2]   Four days after this epochal motion, a committee consisting of Jefferson, Franklin, John Adams, Sherman, and Livingston was chosen to embody these sentiments in immortal declaration. [3] After due deliberation, the document was drafted, reported to Congress, and on July 4, 1776, the Declaration of Independence of the United States of America was adopted by unanimous vote. [4]   Franklin, of course, voted affirmatively in his state delegation, which was carried for the measure only by the absence of two of its members.

The task of drafting the Declaration had been intrusted to Jefferson by the other members of the com-

[1] Franklin (Smyth), VII, 47.
[2] Ford, *Journals of the Continental Congress*, V, 425.
[3] Ibid., p. 431.
[4] Ibid., p. 510.

mittee, and in its final form the document is substantially his.   Franklin seems to have introduced
eleven changes in Jefferson's first draft, most of them
purely verbal and tending toward greater clarity and
emphasis of statement.[1]   One change, however, is of
unparalleled significance.   Where Jefferson, with too
much doubt, perhaps, of what Congress would really
do, had written: "they should declare the causes
which impel them to threaten separation," Franklin
resolutely smashed out the hesitant "threaten" and
wrote a firm "the" in its stead.   It is one of the ironies
of history that he, who had done so much to
strengthen the imperial bond, was destined, by this
stroke of the pen, to set the seal of finality upon
irrevocable separation.

Having taken an unequivocal stand upon this
fundamental point, Franklin seems to have been little
concerned with the precise form which the Declaration might take.   An analysis of the document, however, indicates that it contained nothing inconsistent
with his political creed.   As a declaration of independence of the King, not of Parliament, it was
wholly consistent with Franklin's imperial theory as
manifested in its last stage of development.   In its
conception of the rights of man and the nature of
government, the Declaration closely followed Locke,
and presented nothing which had not become mere

[1] Until recently, it was believed that Franklin was responsible for only
five changes in the original draft.   (Cf. Becker, *The Declaration of Independence,* pp. 161-169.)   A recent study of the original manuscript, however,
indicates eleven emendations made in his handwriting.   (Fitzpatrick, *The
Spirit of the Revolution,* pp. 11-13.)

political platitudes for all good revolutionists. As to the burning indictment of George III which it contained, Franklin had long since changed his opinion of that monarch, whom he now detested with all the hatred which follows unrequited love.[1]

Once having signed the Declaration, and having commented upon the relative merits of collective and individual hanging, Franklin was not a man to turn backward. He would have been well content to live and die under the English flag, had that been possible, but the time had come when the price demanded for that privilege had become too great. He looked upon the Revolution as a war against tyranny, a conflict fought for the fundamental liberties of the human race and involving the rights of Americans and Englishmen alike.[2] He wrote to a friend, "Happy should I have been, if the honest warnings I gave of the fatal separation of interests, as well as of affections, that must attend the measures commenced while I was in England, had been attended to, and the horrid mischief of this abominable war been thereby prevented," but, he concludes, "as to our submitting to the government of Great Britain, it is vain to think of it." [3] For Englishmen who would talk of peace on a basis of dependency, he had only one answer: "We only tell you, that you can have no treaty with us but as an independent state. . . . Your Parliament never

[1] Cf. John Adams' statement that "in all his (Franklin's) conversation, and in all his writings, when he could naturally, and sometimes when he could not, he mentioned the King with great asperity." (Adams, *Works*, III, 178.)

[2] Franklin (Smyth), IX, 350.

[3] Franklin (Smyth), VII, 69.

petual Union for the establishment of the "United Colonies of North America." [1] The event proved that Franklin was once more ahead of his time. Jefferson highly approved the plan,[2] but more timid members feared that a discussion of it would tend to remove all possibility of reconciliation. Without expressing either approbation or disapprobation of it, the measure was quietly permitted to lie upon the table, and was never reintroduced.[3]

According to Franklin's plan, the colonies were to be united into a "firm League of Friendship," with their common interests vested in a general Congress. One delegate was to be allowed for every 5,000 male polls between the ages of sixteen and sixty, and voting was to be by individuals, not by states. The Congress was to have control over foreign affairs, intercolonial relations, general commerce and currency, Indian affairs, and the common military forces. Taxes were to be levied upon the states on the same basis as representation. The executive power was vested in an Executive Council of twelve, appointed by Congress out of its own membership. Members of this Council were to be chosen for a three year term, one third of the number annually, and were not eligible for immediate reëlection. As has been mentioned, the door was left open for reconciliation with Great Britain; otherwise the Union was to be perpetual.

[1] For text of plan see Ford, *Journals of the Continental Congress*, II, 195-199, or Franklin (Smyth), VI, 420-424.

[2] Jefferson, *Works* (1905 ed.), V, 199.

[3] There is no record in the *Journals* of any discussion on the subject of confederation from July 21, 1775, when Franklin submitted his plan, until June 7, 1776.

Perhaps the most striking feature of the government which Franklin here proposes is its remarkable similarity to the New England Confederation of 1643; the resemblance is so close that it can be attributed only to conscious imitation.[1] His only radical departure from this earliest attempt at colonial union is in the retention of the principle of proportional representation which had been a feature of the Albany Plan. In most respects, however, he departs very little from the constitutional structure erected a century and a quarter before.

Although closely following the outlines of the New England Confederation, Franklin is no less loyal to the principles of the Albany Plan. The most marked innovation is in organization of the executive department. Freed from the necessity of placating a jealous Crown, he was able to indulge his obvious preference for an executive council dependent on the legislature. Just what was the source of this preference cannot be determined with exactness. It cannot be attributed to the example of the British Parliament, for Franklin shared the generally accepted belief that in the English system the executive and legislative departments were independent.[2] A philosophical basis for this belief might be found in Locke's advocacy of legislative superiority,[3] but in all probability, Franklin's dominant motive was to avoid that condition of

[1] For a comparative analysis of the two constitutions see *American Political Science Review*, VIII, 406-411.

[2] Cf. Franklin's statement that, "he (the King) is the Executive Power in Great Britain." (Franklin's marginal note on Wheelock, *Reflections Moral and Political on Great Britain and Her Colonies*, p. 26.)

[3] Locke, *Two Treatises of Government*, II, sec. 149.

divided counsels in time of war, of which Pennsylvania's proprietary government had afforded him so tragic an example.   With the elimination of the functions of the Crown, the powers of Congress were of necessity greater than those which he had earlier assigned to the Grand Council.   Franklin's Articles of Confederation also carry the democratic principle one step farther by basing representation upon population instead of financial support.   Another innovation is a provision for possible amendments to the Articles; a very necessary precaution which had been neglected in the preceding frame of government.   With these exceptions, the plan is substantially a reproduction of the preceding proposal.

There can be no doubt that the Articles of Confederation which were eventually adopted were profoundly influenced by Franklin's two earlier plans. Franklin's plan of 1775 and the one proposed in 1776 are almost parallel in development, and are identical in most of their respective provisions.[1]   The most significant change made in the latter—the granting to each state of an equal vote—was bitterly opposed by Franklin as long as he remained in Congress.   In a truly prophetic vein, he declared, "Let the smaller colonies give equal money and men, and then have an equal vote.   But if they have an equal vote without bearing equal burdens, a confederation upon such iniquitous principles will not last long." [2]   As Presi-

---

[1] For the latter plan, see Ford, *Journals*, XIX, 214-222.
[2] Reported in John Adams, *Works*, 496.

dent of the Pennsylvania Convention, he actually prepared a resolution declaring the dissent of the state to these Articles on the grounds that equal representation was incompatible with the essential principles of democratic government. Only the firm-rooted conviction that any form of confederation was better than none induced him to withhold this resolution.[1] It must be remembered, however, that in maintaining the principle of proportional representation, he was speaking not merely as a devotee of abstract justice, but as a representative of one of the richest and most populous states, which naturally had most to gain by that system.

All three of these plans of union, two of them drafted by Franklin, and the third bearing the unmistakable stamp of his influence, prove conclusively that at this time he had no conception of such a frame of government as was evolved by the Federal Constitutional Convention twelve years later. It simply had not occurred to him that a Federal state, as well as a monarchy, might be divided into three departments, executive, legislative, and judicial.[2] Instead, he merely reproduced the familiar form of a federal league with all its powers vested and confused in a one-chamber assembly. His government would have been considerably stronger than the Confederation of the "critical period," but like the latter, it lacked the

[1] Ford, *Journals*, V, 555n.
[2] Cf. John Adams' declaration that "I was the first member of Congress who ventured to come out in public . . . in favor of a government in three branches, with an independent judiciary. . . . Franklin leaned against it." (Adams, *Works*, IX, 617.)

important powers of direct taxation and jurisdiction over the individual. Thus Franklin lost the golden opportunity to become the pioneer in the field of constitutional development that he was in so many other realms of human activity.

Chapter IX

FRANKLIN AND THE PENNSYLVANIA CONSTITUTION

DURING the summer of 1776, another important body was in session in Philadelphia. This was the Constitutional Convention of Pennsylvania which had been called to draft a frame of government for the new state. It was inevitable that the Convention should choose Franklin as its President. The choice, in a sense, was unfortunate; for as presiding officer, Franklin could contribute little to the deliberations, except by giving the prestige of his name to the proceedings.[1]

The part actually taken by Franklin in framing the constitution is not definitely known. George Bryan, who led the majority faction, and James Cannon, who supervised the actual drafting, undoubtedly exerted more influence than he did.[2] John Adams, who had nothing but contempt for Franklin's ability as a political scientist, declared, "He (Franklin) did not even make the constitution of Pennsylvania, bad as it is. The bill of rights is taken almost verbatim from that of Virginia. That of Pennsylvania was written by Timothy Matlack, James Cannon, Thomas Young and Thomas Paine." [3] Making all due allowance for

[1] For minutes of the convention see Force, *American Archives,* 5th series, II, 51-59.
[2] Konkle, *George Bryan and the Const. of Penn.,* p. 126.
[3] Adams, *Works,* III, 220.

57

the unrelenting prejudices of the writer, it is probably safe to say that Franklin's influence was not nearly so great as was believed by many of his admirers, particularly in France. At the same time, it is known that Franklin approved its general principles and later in life defended it when a change was contemplated. For this reason, the constitution of Pennsylvania must be considered as throwing some light upon his political theories.

The single legislative body for which the constitution provided has usually been attributed to Franklin's influence.[1] There is no doubt that this was a favorite principle with Franklin. In arguing for a single legislature, he wrote, "Have we not experienced in this Colony, when a Province under the Government of the Proprietors, the Mischiefs of a second Branch existing in the Proprietary Family, countenanced and aided by an Aristocratic Council?"[2] He feared that if the wisdom of the members be divided into two branches, "may it not be too weak in each to support a good Measure, or obstruct a bad one?"[3] He also opposed as undemocratic the distinction, customary in bicameral legislatures, between the upper

[1] Rochefoucauld wrote, "Franklin was the first who dared to put this idea in practice. The respect which the Pennsylvanians entertained for him induced them to adopt it." (Cited in *Works of Franklin,* ed. Sparks, I, 410.) A pamphleteer of the time, while not ascribing the origin of that feature to him, says that both he and Rittenhouse supported it in the convention, and then adds, "Divine Providence seems to have permitted them to err upon this subject in order to console the world for the very great superiority they both possess over the rest of mankind in everything else except the science of government." (*Observations on the Present Government of Pennsylvania,* p. 12.)

[2] Franklin (Smyth), X, 56.

[3] Ibid., 57.

and lower house, particularly where the upper house was elected under a high property qualification.[1] It is probable, however, that the single assembly would have been accepted even without Franklin's influence. For three quarters of a century, the unicameral system had existed in Pennsylvania under the constitution of 1701; the long struggle to prevent the proprietary executive council from assuming the powers of a second chamber was fresh in the minds of all; and by most of the delegates, the superiority of the single body was regarded as a settled, established fact.[2]

The Pennsylvania Constitution also provided for a single executive, chosen annually by the assembly, who presided over an executive council elected by the people. Franklin believed that this executive should be kept closely responsible to the people, lest there develop a tendency toward an arbitrary hereditary government.[3] To this end, he favored the provision for the popularly elected executive council, which might serve as a check upon him. As will be brought out even more clearly in a study of the Federal Convention, Franklin seems to have had a morbid

[1] Franklin (Smyth), X, 59. In view of such expressions, the following extract from the papers of Dr. Rush is utterly incomprehensible. "It is true, he (Franklin) assented to it (Pennsylvania constitution) but it is equally true, in a letter to General Wayne and in a conversation with Mr. John Morton and myself, he strongly reprobated that part of the constitution which places the Supreme power of the state in the hands of a Single legislature. There is a pamphlet of the Doctor's printed in the year 1763, in which he supposes three branches preferable to two." (Penn. Mag. of Hist., XXIX, 29.) No such letter or pamphlet has been found, nor can these sentiments be reconciled with the repeated statements of Franklin himself.

[2] Konkle, George Bryan and the Const. of Penn., p. 118.

[3] Franklin (Smyth), X, 54.

fear that democracy, unless most carefully safeguarded, would almost inevitably evolve into absolutism.[1]   Such belief was not unnatural in one who
had watched at close range the evolution of British
government during the third quarter of the eighteenth century.

One section of the constitution, if not written by
Franklin, might very well have been.   It was provided that "if any man is called into public service
to the prejudice of his private affairs, he has a right
to a reasonable compensation; and whenever an office,
through increase of fees or otherwise, becomes so
profitable as to occasion many to apply for it, the
profits ought to be lessened."   Franklin consistently
maintained this principle, whereby the ambitious and
avaricious should be resolutely excluded from public
office.   He laid all the ills of Britain to "the enormous
salaries, emoluments, and patronage of great offices,"
which drove men irresistibly into "factions, cabals,
dissensions, and violent divisions, always mischievous
to public councils, destructive to the peace of society,
and sometimes fatal to its existence." [2]   It was Franklin's fixed determination that no such abuses should
find a footing upon this side of the Atlantic.

It would be too much to expect that all parts of
the constitution were acceptable to Franklin.   According to one of its provisions, members of the legislature were required to take an oath affirming belief
in God, in future rewards and punishments, and in

[1] Cf. Chapter XI, infra.
[2] Franklin (Smyth), IX, 169-170.

the divine inspiration of the scriptures. Franklin believed that the latter clause, at least, should have been omitted, but being overwhelmed by numbers, contented himself with inserting the additional provision "that no further or more extended Profession of Faith should ever be exacted." [1] Although no other objections were noted by Franklin, himself, there were undoubtedly other clauses which did not meet his complete approval. It is not probable, for instance, that he approved the provision by which slavery was recognized as a legal institution in Pennsylvania, but with his usual recognition of the imperfect nature of all human institutions, he was ready to accept the lesser evil for the sake of the greater good, and until his death actively supported a constitution which in actual use proved none too popular.

[1] Franklin (Smyth), IX, 266.

Chapter X

FRANKLIN AND THE PHYSIOCRATS

On October 26, 1776, Franklin embarked to take up the tremendous responsibilities of American minister plenipotentiary to the court of France. When, on December 7, he stepped ashore at Nantes, he was received with such nationwide love and veneration as have been accorded to few Americans by a foreign people. Not the least enthusiastic of his welcomers were the members of the French school of economic-political philosophers, the Physiocrats.

Franklin had first become acquainted with these thinkers during his short visit to France in 1767. At that time he met such leaders of the movement as Dupont de Nemours, Mirabeau, Turgot, the Abbé Morellet, Condorcet, and "the venerable apostle Quesnay," himself.[1] Many of Franklin's political and economic ideas can be traced to the influence of these men at this time. During the intervening years, a steady correspondence had been maintained, so that his return was hailed with all the delight of a family reunion. He was enthusiastically admitted to the Lodge of the Nine Sisters, an organization of serious thinkers, united by their common interest in constitutional questions.[2] In this body he exchanged ideas

[1] *The Freeman*, October 24, 1923.
[2] *American Historical Review*, XXI, 713.

with some of the most eminent and original thinkers of his day. Although the interest of this group was essentially economic, the commerce of a nation is so closely related to its government that no study of Franklin's political theories would be complete without a consideration of their influence upon his thought.

The Physiocrats held that the end of the body politic is to extend the enjoyment of the natural rights of liberty and property. They saw that the greater the freedom of intercourse, the greater the possibilities of coöperation and combination by which the production of wealth may be increased and human wants be more easily satisfied. The rights of the individual must be fully safeguarded, insofar as is compatible with the rights of all other individuals. To protect these mutual rights, a strong central government is necessary, preferably a hereditary monarchy. Their theory was in all essentials, the doctrine of "laissez faire," thus fully developed some years before Adam Smith gave it universal currency in his *Inquiry into the Nature and Causes of the Wealth of Nations.*

While Franklin could no longer accept their reasoning in favor of monarchy, he adopted without question their views concerning international relations.[1] His vision was truly international in scope, and he delighted in their freedom from local and na-

[1] In speaking of foreigners whose belief ran parallel to that of the Physiocrats, Dupont wrote, "Who does not know that the English have to-day their Benjamin Franklin, who has adopted the principles and the doctrines of our French Economists, a doctrine that he is so worthy to spread and to defend." (Cited in *The Freeman*, October 24, 1923.)

tional prejudices and partialities.[1] On the subject of free trade, he wrote, "I find myself rather inclin'd to adopt that modern one, which supposes it best for every Country to leave its Trade entirely free from all Incumbrances,"[2] and again, "In general, I would only observe that commerce, consisting in a mutual exchange of the necessities and conveniences of life, the more free and unrestrained it is, the more it flourishes; and the happier are all the nations concerned in it."[3] He believed that governmental interference in the price of commodities was contrary to the very nature of commerce, and lamented that ignorance or self-interest so frequently led princes and parliaments to sacrifice their real welfare to the greed for immediate gain.[4] On this theme, he wrote, "If we may judge by the acts, arrêts, and edicts, all the world over, for regulating commerce, an assembly of great men is the greatest fool upon earth."[5] "In time, perhaps, Mankind may be wise enough to let Trade take its own Course, find its own Channels, and regulate its own Proportions."[6] At another time, he wrote to Dupont, lamenting the fact that the "wisdom which sees the welfare of the parts in the prosperity of the whole" seems not yet to be known in England, where it is not suspected "that what is best for mankind, or even for Europe in general, may be best for us."[7]

Franklin, although reaching the same goal, advo-

---

[1] Cf. Chapter XIII, infra.
[2] Franklin (Smyth), VIII, 261.
[3] Franklin (Smyth), IX, 19.
[4] Franklin (Smyth), IV, 469.

[5] Franklin (Smyth), IX, 241.
[6] Franklin (Smyth), IV, 243.
[7] Franklin (Smyth), V, 155.

cated free trade upon slightly different grounds than did the Physiocrats and Adam Smith. The latter, in their arguments, emphasized the natural right of man to the free disposal of the product of his own labor.[1] Franklin, on the other hand, believed that all property beyond that necessary for the preservation and propagation of the race was the property of the state which had created it.[2] He believed trade restrictions reprehensible because human experience had shown such measures to be an unwise economic policy. To put the distinction with perfect bluntness, Adam Smith denounced trade restriction because it was unjust; Franklin opposed it because it was unprofitable. But whatever his motives, Franklin deserves infinite credit for grasping a truth which few men of his day comprehended, and which, if rightly understood, might have saved to England her American colonies.

[1] Cf. Adam Smith's statement that "to prohibit a great people . . . from making all that they can of every part of their products, or from employing their stock and industry in the way that they judge most advantageous to themselves, is a manifest violation of the most sacred rights of mankind." (Smith, *Wealth of Nations*, 1904 ed., II, 83.)

[2] Cf. page 8, supra.

Chapter XI

FRANKLIN AND THE FEDERAL CONVENTION

THE period of Franklin's ministry to France shows a distinct broadening of his political interests. Doctrines which he had applied to problems of domestic, or at the most, of imperial concern, were turned into the wider field of international relationships. Since this phase of Franklin's political philosophy represents the most highly developed and the most universal application of his political belief, it is altogether fitting that it be left for final consideration. We shall, therefore, pass on to the scene of his last great contribution to the constitutional history of America, the Federal Convention of 1787.

It was only just that Franklin should have lived to assist in the final establishment of the new nation to which so great a portion of his life had been devoted. For the purpose of this study, it can only be regretted that the feebleness of his eighty-one years prevented him from taking a leading part in the deliberations.[1] So far as Franklin's political theories are concerned, it represents the final stage of the evolutionary process; the final verdict, with the evidence all in.

[1] Franklin's weakness was purely physical. William Pierce, a delegate from Georgia, wrote, "He (Franklin) is 82 years old, and possesses an activity of mind equal to a youth of 25 years of age." (*The Records of the Federal Conv.*, ed. Farrand, III, 328.)

Moreover, for frankness of debate and comparative freedom from the restrictions of precedent, the proceedings of the convention are unique. For these reasons, everything which Franklin said there takes on an added significance. If it is impossible to reconstruct from his part in the proceedings the complete system of Franklin's political philosophy, there are at least certain isolated expressions of belief which may serve to throw additional light upon the whole.

The membership of the constitutional convention may be roughly divided into three groups. At the two extremes were those who favored a strong central union and those who advocated a looser confederation in which state rights were to be carefully safeguarded. In between were the men who, when agreement seemed all but impossible, stepped into the breach and by a series of compromises gave to the constitution its final form. Wherever may have been his sympathies, Franklin's natural disposition early led him to ally himself with the latter group. No other episode in Franklin's life serves better to illustrate the fact that a practical working system rather than an absolutely perfect one was the goal of his political philosophy.

There is evidence, however, that Franklin shared the vision of a strong national union as held by Hamilton, Madison, Wilson, and Gouverneur Morris. Throughout his life he had clung fast to the principle that in the body politic the best interests of the parts are inseparably bound up in the well-being of the whole. In discussing the question of representation,

he declared that "it would be better if every Member
of Congress . . . were to consider himself rather as
a Representative of the whole, than as an Agent for
the Interests of a particular State." [1]   The hope was
a vain one, and Franklin soon recognized it to be such,
but it shows that his spirit of broad nationalism had
risen above the narrow limits of sectional and local interest to a conception of a united nation in which the
whole was indeed greater than any of its parts.   He
utterly rejected Montesquieu's dictum that republican government can not be applied over a large terri-
tory.[2]   The same recognition of national supremacy
reveals itself in Franklin's motion that "the national
legislature ought to be empowered to negative all
laws, passed by the several states, contravening, in the
opinion of the national legislature, the articles of
union or any treaties subsisting under the authority
of the union." [3]   Had this resolution found a place in
the constitution, it would both have vested a tremendous power in the national legislature and have at
once resolved the still unsettled question of the
validity of state legislation which conflicts with
treaty obligations.[4]   It apparently never occurred to
him that the power to pass upon the constitutionality
not only of state but also of federal legislation might

[1] Franklin (Smyth), IX, 596.
[2] Franklin (Smyth), IV, 55.   Cf. Montesquieu, *Spirit of Laws*, VIII, 16.
[3] *The Records of the Federal Conv.*, ed. Farrand, I, 47.
[4] For example, the California anti-Japanese legislation of recent years,
which has at times brought forth vigorous and perhaps not unjust protest
from the Japanese government.   Where the offending state law concerns an
internal question such as education, the right of the Supreme Court to
declare it null and void is still controversial.

be vested in the judiciary. If it had, he probably would have denied the right of so small and independent a body to nullify the popular will.

Perhaps the most bitter of the many debates which marked the secret proceedings of the convention was that concerning the basis of representation in the national legislature. Franklin fully understood the fundamental issues of the controversy. "If a proportional representation takes place," he said, "the small States contend that their liberties will be in danger. If an equality of votes is to be put in its place, the large States say their money will be in danger." [1] Franklin's personal preference would have been for a single house in which the number of representatives "should bear some proportion to the number of the represented." [2] A year after the convention, he wrote to a friend that he still believed that a single chamber would have been preferable.[3] In the convention, the only vote against a bicameral legislature was given by Pennsylvania, "probably from complaisance to Dr. Franklin who was understood to be partial to a single house." [4] He accepted the verdict of the convention without question, and with characteristic adaptability set about finding a division of

[1] *The Records of the Federal Conv.*, ed. Farrand, I, 488.
[2] Ibid., I, 197; III, 170.
[3] Franklin (Smyth), IX, 674.
[4] *The Records of the Federal Conv.*, ed. Farrand, I, 48. Franklin's advocacy of this feature, resting though it did upon the sound basis of logic and experience, was curiously unpopular with contemporary leaders. John Adams declared, "No country ever will be long happy or ever entirely safe and free which is thus governed. The curse of a *jus vagum* will be their portion." (Adams, *Works*, IX, 429.) For Hamilton's views, see *The Federalist*, No. 61.

powers and basis of representation in the two houses which would be acceptable to both large and small states.[1]

There is evidence that Franklin would have approved a system of proportional representation in both houses of Congress.[2] He was too wise a political general, however, to insist upon the impossible. On June 30, he proposed what seemed to him to be an equitable basis for compromise. By his plan, each state was to have equal representation in the second house; in all questions touching the sovereignty of the states or increasing the authority of the general government, and in the appointment of civil officers, each state was to have equal suffrage; but in money bills the delegates of the several states were to have suffrage in proportion to the contributions of their states to the common treasury.[3] Two days after this plan was presented, Franklin was appointed to represent Pennsylvania upon the grand committee which had been chosen to effect a compromise when all other means of agreement had failed.[4] By this committee, Franklin's plan was made the basis for discussion, and with certain modifications was reported to the con-

---

[1] Franklin had already presented a plan of compromise based upon a unicameral legislative system. Each state was to make equal contributions to the support of the government and was to enjoy equal representation. Extraordinary demands were to be met by voluntary contributions of the larger states. (Franklin (Smyth), IX, 598-599.) With the decision in favor of a bicameral legislature, the plan fell into well-merited oblivion. It is of interest chiefly as a revival of Franklin's old faith in requisitions, in which he had placed so much trust during the Stamp Act controversy.

[2] *The Records of the Federal Conv.*, ed. Farrand, III, 152.

[3] Franklin (Smyth), IX, 602.

[4] *The Records of the Federal Conv.*, ed. Farrand, II, 12.

vention in the form now familiar to all Americans.[1] It is thus one of the ironies of history that Franklin, who consistently opposed the bicameral legislature, should have been so instrumental in giving it an enduring place in the American system of government.

So far as Franklin is concerned, this debate is significant for his consistent advocacy of a unicameral legislature based upon proportional representation, both of which are devices for giving a large measure of freedom to the sovereign voice of the people. By supporting these measures Franklin revealed himself as a champion of democracy in a body in which the aristocratic impulse was by no means lacking. So far as he was concerned, however, they were old principles which had been embodied in the Albany Plan of Union some thirty-three years before.

The question of representation having been disposed of, the convention turned to the equally delicate problem of the national executive. With fearful and uncertain steps, the delegates approached a subject so reminiscent of a tyrannical monarch and arbitrary royal governors. The great lesson which they derived from history was that government always tends to become oppressive, and that the great engine of oppression is the executive department. With no precedent to guide them, it was no easy task to create an administrative organ which would safely function in that uncertain ground which lies between impotence and oppression.

[1] *The Records of the Federal Conv.*, ed. Farrand, I, 523.

Franklin seems to have shared the quite general belief that a single executive would be but a stepping stone upon the road to monarchy.[1] In explanation of his fears he said, "There is a natural inclination in mankind to Kingly Government.[2] It sometimes relieves them from Aristocratic domination. They had rather have one tyrant than five hundred.[3] It gives more of the appearance of equality among Citizens, and that they like. I am apprehensive therefore, perhaps too apprehensive, that the Government of these States, may in future times, end in a Monarchy."[4] He therefore advocated an executive council which would "not only be a check on a bad President but be a relief to a good one."[5] Such a body, appointed by the legislature, would not only exert a moderating influence upon the president, but would insure continuity in case of his illness or death.[6] Although the proposal had the support of such leaders as Wilson, Dickinson, and Madison, the measure was ultimately rejected.

As a further check upon the malignant growth of personal ambition, Franklin moved that the Executive

[1] The popular anxiety upon this point is indicated by Hamilton in *The Federalist*, No. 66.

[2] Rousseau, also, thought he saw this ceaseless tendency in government to contract itself from democracy to aristocracy and thence to monarchy. (Rousseau, *Social Contract*, III, 10.) It is probable, however, that Franklin's view was derived from his study of history, rather than from the pages of that philosopher.

[3] Franklin, himself, believed that the arbitrary government of a single person would be preferable to the arbitrary government of a body of men, since the former might be restrained by a sense of fear or shame. (Franklin (Bigelow), IV, 311.)

[4] *The Records of the Federal Conv.*, ed. Farrand, I, 83.

[5] Ibid., II, 542.

[6] Franklin (Smyth), IX, 603.

should receive, beyond his necessary expenses, "no salary, stipend, fee or reward whatsoever." [1] Thus he hoped to remove the office from the clutch of greed and avarice. Nor did he believe that men would be wanting who would find that "the pleasure of doing good and serving their Country and the respect such conduct entitles them to are sufficient motives . . . to give up a great portion of their time to the Public, without the mean inducement of pecuniary satisfaction." [2] If for once the practical Franklin might seem to verge upon the Utopian, it must be said that in his own long life of public service the question of remuneration was always held subordinate. Acting on the same principle that offices of profit are a constant menace to republican institutions, he favored the motion "that no Salary should be allowed" [3] members of the Senate, and had the compensation of the national legislators changed from "liberal" to "moderate." [4] At the same time, he recognized that fixed and adequate salaries must be paid judges if a free and independent judiciary was to be maintained. [5]

It seems probable, to judge from a somewhat ambiguous entry in Madison's "Journal," that Franklin favored the proposition that the executive be chosen for seven years and be ineligible for reëlection. [6] He seems, however, to have had no serious objection to

[1] *The Records of the Federal Conv.*, ed. Farrand, I, 78.
[2] Cf. Montesquieu's belief that in republics service in public employment should be compulsory. (*Spirit of Laws*, V, 19.)
[3] *The Records of the Federal Conv.*, ed. Farrand, I, 426.
[4] Ibid., I, 216.
[5] Ibid., I, 84; II, 44.
[6] Ibid., II, 120.

the four-year term with possibility of reëlection, so long as the proper safeguards against abuse of power were observed.[1]   To this end, he opposed giving the president an absolute veto, which he thought might readily be converted into a weapon of coercion and oppression.[2]   It did not seem logical to him "that one man can possess more wisdom than both branches of the legislature."[3]   Instead, he believed that a mere suspensory veto would be sufficient to safeguard against hasty and ill-considered legislative action.[4] He favored a system of impeachment, as providing "for the regular punishment of the Executive if he should deserve it, and for his honorable acquittal if he should be unjustly accused."[5]

Experience has shown that many of the restrictions advocated by Franklin were unnecessary. They are significant, however, as indicating his belief that political liberty rested upon the exaltation of the function and position of the legislature, accompanied by a corresponding depression of the powers of the executive. He clearly did not share the belief held by John Adams, Hamilton, and even Jefferson, that the greatest danger to liberty lay in the expanding power of the legislative body.[6]   Franklin believed that "in free Governments the rulers are the servants, and the people their superiors and sovereigns,"[7] and all

[1] Franklin (Smyth), IX, 674.
[2] *The Records of the Federal Conv.*, ed. Farrand, I, 99.
[3] Ibid., I, 106.
[4] Ibid., I, 94.
[5] Ibid., II, 65.
[6] Cf. Adams, *Works*, VI, 7; *The Federalist*, No. 70; Jefferson, *Writings*, V, 83.
[7] *The Records of the Federal Conv.*, ed. Farrand, II, 120.

his activities in the convention were devoted to the end that this fundamental relationship should not be destroyed.

Although many of Franklin's favorite theories had been rejected, he strongly favored the acceptance of the proposed draft.[1] Rather than to reject it for its seeming imperfections, he urged each of his colleagues "to doubt a little of his own infallibility."[2] At the same time, he recognized that which many of the patriot leaders failed to understand; that government to be effective must be a government of men as well as of laws.[3] "I think," he declared, "there is no form of Government but what may be a blessing to the people if well administered and believe farther that this is likely to be well administered for a course of years and can only end in Despotism, as other forms have done before it, when the people shall become so corrupted as to need despotic Government, being incapable of any other."[4] Thus he realized that it is the spirit and temper of the people in which confidence must be placed, rather than the written word embodied in an instrument of government. In the last analysis, therefore, he realized that democratic

[1] He wrote to Le Veillard, "I am of opinion with you, that the two chambers were not necessary, and I disliked some other articles that are in, and wished for some that are not in the proposed plan. I nevertheless hope it may be adopted." (Franklin (Smyth), IX, 645.)

[2] Franklin (Smyth), IX, 609.

[3] For example, the constitution of Massachusetts provided for a rigid separation of powers "to the end that it may be a government of laws and not of men." (Poore, *The Federal and State Constitutions*, I, 960.)

[4] Jefferson foresaw much the same evolutionary process. He believed that Americans would continue to be virtuous and retain their democratic form of government as long as they remained an agricultural people, but "when they get piled upon one another in large cities as in Europe, they will become corrupt as in Europe." (Jefferson, *Writings*, IV, 479.)

government can only be justified by attributing to man the innate capacity for self-government. The question naturally rises, whether in his foreboding of ultimate despotism he does not imply a fatal distrust of democratic government.

Chapter XII

FRANKLIN AND DEMOCRACY

FRANKLIN is usually regarded as the earliest outstanding American exponent of the democratic principle. In the sense that democracy presupposes the existence of a people enjoying equality of rights without hereditary or arbitrary differences in rank or privilege, this view is undoubtedly correct. Nor can there be any doubt of his belief that, somehow, the sovereign power ought to be vested in this people. At the same time, there is evidence that he accepted not without some misgiving man's capacity for self-government. His political views may be said to combine an unqualified acceptance of the democratic ideal with a certain distrust of its practicability as applied to actual government. In justice to Franklin, it should be remembered that the representative governments of the eighteenth century were in no sense of the word Utopian.

Franklin fully accepted the Revolutionary principle that all men are endowed with certain inalienable rights which are inherent in the very essence of government. He declared, "The important ends of Civil Society, and the personal Securities of Life and Liberty, these remain the same in every Member of

77

the society; and the poorest continues to have an equal Claim to them with the most opulent." [1] One of his strongest objections to the bicameral legislative system was that wealth and privilege customarily enjoyed a disproportionate influence in one of the houses. He opposed all forms of primogeniture as inconsistent with this principle of human equality.[2] It is not surprising, therefore, to find him among those who severely criticized the hereditary features of the Order of the Cincinnati.[3] During the War of Independence, a reconciliation was proposed to him upon the basis that "America should be governed by a Congress of American peers, to be created and appointed by the King," for which honor Franklin, Washington, Adams and Hancock were specifically mentioned.[4] The vigor with which Franklin repudiated this badge of "everlasting infamy" brought joy to the soul of so stern a critic as John Adams.[5] As for hereditary legislators, Franklin saw "more Propriety, because less Hazard of Mischief, in having Hereditary Professors of Mathematics." [6]

Such absolute denial of all forms of hereditary privilege would seem necessarily to imply an opposition to hereditary monarchy. It is surprising, therefore, to see by what a slow evolutionary process Franklin came to accept this seemingly obvious corollary. Absolutism of any kind was repugnant to him, but for the greater part of his life he maintained the

[1] Franklin (Smyth), X, 59-60.
[2] Franklin (Smyth), VIII, 421.
[3] Franklin (Smyth), IX, 161.
[4] Adams, *Works*, III, 178.
[5] Franklin (Smyth), VII, 172.
[6] Franklin (Smyth), VI, 371.

superiority of a properly limited constitutional monarchy. His early enthusiasm for the British system
has already been noted.[1] Shortly before the Revolution, when bitter experience had begun to weaken his
instinctive and deep-seated reverence for his King,
he wrote, "I am not quite satisfied of the necessity or
utility of that office in Great Britain, as I see many
flourishing states in the world governed well and
happy without it."[2] With the outbreak of hostilities,
this feeling of uncertainty soon gave place to an in-
tense antipathy toward all things monarchic. When,
in the darkest days of the Revolution, it was proposed
that dictatorial powers be conferred upon Washington, Franklin and his adherents strongly opposed the
measure.[3] The vigor with which he resisted all monarchic tendencies in the Federal Convention has already been mentioned and is indicative of the most
complete alienation of his earlier sympathies.

In his early days, Franklin does not seem to have
believed that universal suffrage was essential to the
maintenance of the rights of the individual. On this
subject he wrote, "As to those who have no landed
property . . . the allowing them to vote for legislators is an impropriety."[4] Nor do his early writings
exhibit any marked concern over the gross injustices
of the English electoral system. Not until the ap-
proaching Revolution finally drove him from the
arms of King and Parliament into the embrace of the
people, did he accept the principle that "the fran-

[1] Cf. Page 36, supra.
[2] Franklin (Bigelow), IV, 78.
[3] *Facsimiles*, ed. Stevens, No. 737, p. 2.
[4] Franklin (Bigelow), III, 496.

chise is the common right of freemen." [1] However, he specifically excluded from the exercise of this political right "minors, servants, and others, who are liable to undue influence." [2] Woman's suffrage was, of course, an undreamed of innovation in Franklin's day. In the Federal Convention, he gave a practical demonstration of his more liberal later belief, when he vigorously opposed a proposal to limit the suffrage to freeholders. He declared that such a measure would injure the community as a whole by tending to lower the tone, spirit, and courage of the poorer classes. [3] His attitude on this point is all the more significant when it is recalled that at this time the actual voting constituency of the States included less than one half of the adult white male population. [4]

Writers like Milton and Algernon Sydney seem to have reinforced his natural inclination toward liberal forms of government. As has been seen, all the numerous frames of government which he proposed embodied the principles of representative government. In his provisions for extending representative responsibility and for safeguarding the popular will from external aggression, he showed himself in accord with the best democratic traditions of the time. But Franklin had had too much experience with the conflicting prejudices and the resultant compromises of popular assemblies to feel any profound reverence for the "collective wisdom" of the people. "If all officers appointed by governors were always men of

1 Franklin (Smyth), IX, 342.
2 Franklin (Bigelow), VIII, 411.
3 *The Records of the Federal Conv.*, ed. Farrand, II, 205, 208.
4 Merriam, *A History of American Political Theories*, p. 85.

merit," he wrote in 1755, "it would be wrong ever to hazard a popular election."[1] The example of the British Parliament led him to adopt the cynical belief that in popular assemblies the voice of the people was usually silenced by the selfish interests of individuals and parties.[2] Nor did the great body of the people escape his condemnation. The popular indignation which the proposed Federal Constitution aroused in many states, seemed proof to Franklin "that popular Opposition to a public Measure is no Proof of its Impropriety, even tho' the Opposition be excited and headed by Men of Distinction."[3] Again, after the Constitution had been adopted, he wrote, "We have been guarding against an evil that old States are most liable to, *excess of power* in the rulers; but our present danger seems to be *defect of obedience* in the subjects."[4] Thus he expressed doubts which all intelligent observers must feel at times when viewing the blundering ineptitudes and extravagant incompetence with which a free people are wont to govern themselves. But there is another side to the picture, as Franklin would have been the first to recognize. Whatever the defects of democracy, it seemed to him immeasurably better than any other system of government which preceding generations had evolved, and until something better could be shown him, he gave to it his fullest allegiance. It is perhaps a fair evaluation of Franklin's attitude to say that if he did not share Jefferson's reverent belief in the popular capacity for self-government, neither did he share the

[1] Franklin (Smyth), III, 309.
[2] Franklin (Smyth), IX, 241.
[3] Ibid., 702.
[4] Franklin (Smyth), X, 7.

cynical unbelief of Hamilton's aristocratic creed. Nor would he have subscribed to John Adams' pessimistic avowal that, "All projects of government, formed upon a supposition of continual vigilance, sagacity, virtue, and firmness of the people, when possessed of the exercise of supreme power, are cheats and delusions." [1]

Franklin's true feelings on this subject are shown in the enthusiasm with which he hailed the dawn of the French Revolution—happily he did not live to see the excesses of the later years of that movement. "God grant," he wrote, "that not only the Love of Liberty, but a thorough Knowledge of the Rights of Man, may pervade all the Nations of the Earth." [2] In the closing years of his life it was a pleasing reflection to him "that liberty, which some years since appeared in danger of extinction, is now regaining the ground she had lost, that arbitrary governments are likely to become more mild and reasonable, and to expire by degrees, giving place to more equitable forms; one of the effects this of the art of printing, which diffuses so general a light, augmenting with the growing day, and of so penetrating a nature, that all the window-shutters despotism and priestcraft can oppose to keep it out, prove insufficient." [3] From this optimistic view of a new world order, it is an easy transition to a consideration of Franklin's political theories as applied to the broad field of international relationships.

[1] Adams, *Works*, VI, 166.
[2] Franklin (Smyth), X, 72.
[3] Franklin (Smyth), IX, 102.

Chapter XIII

FRANKLIN THE INTERNATIONALIST

FRANKLIN lived in a day when nationalism and imperialism seemed linked in an unholy alliance forever to banish peace from the earth. There was scarcely a year of the eighteenth century during which European nations or their colonies were not somewhere engaged in armed conflict, as reputedly civilized princes battled for broader empires and wider spheres of economic control. In the face of so much undisguised greed and shameless aggression, the benevolent philosopher came to adopt the belief that "there has never been, nor ever will be, any such thing as a good War or a bad Peace." [1] No one saw more clearly than he the wasteful futility of war. He wrote, "What vast additions to the Conveniences and Comforts of Living might mankind have acquired, if the Money spent in Wars had been employed in Works of public utility! What an extension of Agriculture, even to the Tops of our Mountains: what Rivers rendered navigable, or joined by Canals: what Bridges, Aqueducts, new Roads, and other public Works, Edifices, and Improvements, rendering England a compleat Paradise, might have been obtained by spending those Millions in doing good,

[1] Franklin (Smyth), XIII, 454.

which in the last War have been spent in doing Mischief; in bringing Misery into thousands of Families, and destroying the Lives of so many thousands of working people, who might have performed the useful labour." [1]   Unlike those who believe that trial by arms is the inevitable final arbiter in human affairs, Franklin was unable to understand why war must be accepted as an inherent attribute of civilized society. "Thank God," he wrote with an optimism as laudable as it was misplaced, "the world is growing wiser and wiser; and as by degrees men are convinced of the folly of wars for religion, for dominion, or for commerce, they will be happier and happier." [2]   So strong was his faith in humanity that he believed that the most frightful anomaly of modern civilization might indeed be abolished, and to that end the later years of his life were in large measure devoted.

As in many other fields, Franklin's ideas concerning national defence were evolutionary in their nature. In 1747, when exhorting the people of Pennsylvania to take measures for the common defence, he repeated the not unfamiliar axiom that "the Way to secure Peace is to be prepared for War." [3]   By 1773, however, he had come to advocate the total abolition of the burdensome system of standing armies. [4]   He believed that this might be accomplished by a common agreement among the powers of Europe.   Thus at that early date, he advanced the principle which not until the Washington Conference of 1921-2 was to

[1] Franklin (Smyth), IX, 74.
[2] Ibid., 657.
[3] Franklin (Smyth), II, 352.
[4] Franklin (Bigelow), VIII, 420.

find a first halting application to international problems.

In place of a blind reliance upon force, Franklin would have put international relations upon the basis, even now not fully understood, that "Justice is as strictly due between neighbor Nations as between neighbor Citizens." [1] On this equitable principle he sought to establish the foreign intercourse of his country. Less than three weeks after Bunker Hill he wrote, "If we must have a War, let it be carried on as between nations who had once been Friends, and wish to be so again." [2] Again, when peace with England was first discussed, he expressed the hope "that there may be wisdom enough assembled to make, if possible, a peace that shall be perpetual, and that the idea of any nations being natural enemies to each other may be abolished, for the honour of human nature." [3] Because of his pacific tendencies, he had not expected to be entrusted with the peace negotiations,[4] and when chosen upon the commission, he made an earnest effort to frame the treaty with Britain upon such terms as would remove all traces of antagonism and jealousy between the two nations.

Franklin believed that the foreign policy of the United States should be carefully devised so as to avoid the perils of stupid isolation upon the one hand and servile dependence upon the other. To those who favored a submissive alliance with this power or that,

[1] Franklin (Smyth), IX, 296.
[2] Unpublished manuscript in library of William S. Mason.
[3] Franklin (Smyth), VIII, 414.
[4] Ibid., 5.

chase for some valuable Consideration, than to think of driving them out by Force, being almost sure it would be cheaper as well as honester." [1]

Franklin was one of the first among great political thinkers to advocate universal and compulsory arbitration for international disputes. While the Revolution was still on, he wrote to his friend, Richard Price, "We make daily great Improvements in Natural, there is one I wish to see in Moral Philosophy; the Discovery of a Plan, that would induce and oblige Nations to settle their Disputes without first Cutting one another's Throats." [2]   Again he wrote, "All Wars are Follies, very expensive, and very mischievous ones. When will Mankind be convinced of this, and agree to settle their Differences by Arbitration?   Were they to do it, even by the Cast of a Dye, it would be better than by Fighting and destroying each other." [3]

It is rather surprising that Franklin, with his characteristic abhorrence of the merely theoretical, did not formulate some practical scheme for making universal peace a reality.   Instead, he was satisfied to give currency to the plan of another. This was *A Project of Universal and Perpetual Peace,* written by Pierre-André Gargaz, a former galley slave, and printed by Franklin upon his private press at Passy. [4] The plan provided for a perpetual congress consisting

[1] Franklin (Smyth), IX, 545.
[2] Franklin (Smyth), VIII, 9.
[3] Franklin (Smyth), IX, 12.
[4] *A Project of Universal and Perpetual Peace Written by Pierre-André Gargaz, a former Galley Slave, and Printed by Benjamin Franklin at Passy in 1782.* Ed. by G. S. Eddy. (New York, 1922.)

of one representative from each nation of Europe. No sovereign was to make any territorial acquisitions unless these be specifically approved by the Congress.[1] If any monarch died without heirs, or conducted illegal war, he was to be replaced by a prince chosen by the Congress, and "each Sovereign of the union shall furnish all the aid that the Congress shall deem proper to establish and maintain in his Sovereignty the Prince whom it shall have chosen."[2] Limitations were to be put upon the size of armies to be maintained by the member states, in time of war as well as in peace. Gargaz then went on to discuss and refute possible objections which might be advanced against the project.[3]

Franklin's personal reaction to this plan was such as might be expected from one who combined so strangely a lofty idealism with a stern utilitarianism. He declared that "though his Project may appear in some respects chimerical,"[4] nevertheless, it "seems to me to contain some very sensible remarks."[5] Anything which would tend to promote international good-feeling was sure of his approval, but he seems to have doubted the efficacy of such an international legislative body as Gargaz suggested. The best expression of Franklin's views on the subject of an inter-

[1] Cf. Article X of the League of Nations Covenant.
[2] Cf. Article XVI of the League of Nations Covenant.
[3] Gargaz' project was by no means original with him. His plan followed very closely the proposed Federation of Europe which had been suggested by Rousseau in 1756. Cf. Rousseau, *A Lasting Peace through the Federation of Europe.* (London, 1917.)
[4] Franklin (Smyth), IX, 46.
[5] Franklin (Bigelow), VIII, 418.

national organization appears in a conversation as reported by one of his friends.[1] "He (Franklin) observed that the plans which he had seen for this purpose were in general impracticable in this respect, viz., that they supposed a general agreement among the sovereigns of Europe to send delegates to a particular place. Now, although perhaps two or three of them might be willing to come into this measure, it is improbable and next to impossible that all, or even a majority of them would do it. But if they would have patience, he thought they might accomplish it, agree upon an alliance against all aggressors, and agree to refer all disputes between each other to some third person, or set of men, or power. Other nations, seeing the advantage of this would gradually accede, and perhaps in one hundred and fifty or two hundred years all Europe would be included."[2] To borrow modern phraseology, Franklin at this time favored a system of territorial guarantees, supplemented by a World Court, rather than the complex machinery of a League of Nations. That Franklin was justified in his fears that national distrust and suspicion would go far to prevent the formation of an effective international agency for peace, no American can deny. Perhaps it was with prophetic insight that in the Federal Convention he opposed the creation of the United States Senate.

In his search for some sure method by which to settle peacefully the differences of nations, the Con-

[1] John Baynes, who visited Franklin in Paris in 1783.
[2] Franklin (Bigelow), VIII, 418.

stitution of the United States came to Franklin as a distinct omen of hope. If the jealousies and conflicting interests of the several states might thus be reconciled in the formation of a general union, he saw no reason why the principle might not be applied in the broader field of international relations. To a European correspondent he wrote, "If it (the new government) succeeds, I do not see why you might not in Europe carry the Project of good Henry the 4th into Execution, by forming a Federal Union and one Grand Republick of all its different States and Kingdoms, by means of a like Convention, for we had many Interests to reconcile." [1] Even the present League of Nations does not carry the federative principle to the extent which Franklin would seem to imply here. However, he does not seem to have contemplated anything more than a European federation; it apparently never entered his mind that some day America would be brought so close to Europe that her participation in such an organization might seem desirable. On the other hand, in view of his abiding passion for human coöperation and his tolerant recognition "that what is best for mankind, or even for Europe in general, may be best for us," [2] there is no reason to believe that he would have opposed American participation in any plan, however faulty, for the better adjustment of international relations.

Although he was among the pioneers in the move-

[1] Franklin (Smyth), IX, 619.
[2] Cf. Page 56, supra.

ment for abolishing war, Franklin did not scorn lesser projects for the alleviation of its hardships. To this end, he favored the abolition of privateering, the exemption of contraband from confiscation, and the freedom of peaceful non-combatants from molestation.[1] Many of these enlightened principles he caused to be inserted in the treaty which he negotiated with Prussia in 1785.[2] One of the provisions of this treaty was the abolition of blockades of every description, a principle of international law which deserved a better fate than the oblivion into which it has fallen. Thus in some respects, Franklin's conception of the law of nations was ahead not only of his time but of our own as well.

[1] Franklin (Smyth), VIII, 82. James Madison called Franklin the "undisputed American Father" of the principle that unarmed merchant vessels of one belligerent should be unmolested by the other. (*Writings* of James Madison, VIII, 283.)

[2] For text of treaty see Malloy, *Treaties,* etc., II, 1477-86. It is of interest to note that in the recent war the German government invoked Article XXIII of this treaty to protest the activities of the United States Alien Property Custodian.

Chapter XIV

FRANKLIN'S THEORIES TO-DAY

IT is perhaps unfair to evaluate an individual's political philosophy in the light of the knowledge and experience of a much later date. That which time has proved to be false, the critic is wont to magnify; while that which has found verification, he is accustomed to minimize as an obvious truth which should have been self-evident. One certainly can not estimate Franklin's worth as a scientist by comparing his views on electricity with the knowledge of an Edison or a Steinmetz. It is perhaps equally unjust to attempt to judge his political belief by the standards of the twentieth century. Unlike the physical sciences, however, the test of time is the only one which can be applied to the formulas of political science. For this reason, a brief consideration of Franklin's ideas as they appear to-day may assist in an understanding of their true significance.

Locke's conception of the fundamental nature of government, which Franklin accepted almost as a matter of course, is no longer commonly held. The social compact theory, with all its corollaries of equality, inalienable rights, and so on, has been replaced by others, resting upon less theoretical sociological and economic conceptions. Time has also proved that the "laissez faire" principles of the Physiocrats are open to fatal economic and social abuses of which Franklin never dreamed. The desirability of free trade is still a debatable question, depending largely upon the geographic location and economic circumstance of the individual.

As has been pointed out, Franklin's conception of the structure of the British Empire has become a reality in the present British commonwealth of nations, united in the traditional person of the English sovereign. Like Franklin's own imperial theory, the British Empire as it is understood to-day has been the product of a long evolutionary process, painfully forced by the exigencies of imperial relations. The constitutional question of imperial trade regulation, which Franklin found so difficult to explain away, seems about to be solved through the medium of the Imperial Conference, an informal body called into being to confer upon problems of empire which are too broad in scope to be handled by the independent action of the constituent assemblies.

Franklin's principles of democracy have more than held their own with the passage of time. It has become literally true, as he once hoped, that "a lover of liberty may find a country in any part of Christendom." [1] Throughout the world his principles of an extended franchise and proportional representation have been steadily gaining ground, as in nation after nation the people have claimed a fuller share in their own government. Franklin would have taken keen

[1] Franklin (Smyth), X, 63.

delight in the Parliamentary Bill of 1911, which marked the beginning of the end for the old House of Lords, with its repugnant system of hereditary legislators. Even his favorite system of a unicameral legislature with responsible executive has been coming into increased favor with the passing years. Nor can it be denied that twentieth century philosophers still occasionally give way to the same misgivings as to man's capacity for self-government which assailed Franklin in the days when representative government was scarcely more than an untried experiment.

It is, however, in the field of international relations that Franklin's vision has had its most dramatic and most tragic vindication. The need for closer international coöperation, which he was among the first to see clearly, is now manifest to almost all. Viewed in the clarifying perspective of a century and a half, this would seem to be his most significant contribution to the political thought of his day. In his conception of the duties and responsibilities of nation to nation, his political theories attain their loftiest and most progressive form. They reveal him as something more than a practical-minded politician; they show that he was also capable of the far-seeing vision of the idealist. The one unwavering principle of his science of government was his steadfast and abiding faith in human coöperation. It is probably true that in its other aspects there was little of the original on Franklin's political philosophy; he was satisfied to be led rather than to lead, and to serve as a mere barometer of popular thought. But in the application of united effort to the common problems of human society, he was consistently in advance of contemporary thought. Coöperation for the common good was with him a religion, more real to him perhaps than any orthodox creed. No system which has been consciously evolved to further this ideal can be far wrong, nor will it become obsolete so long as human society itself endures. On this firm and immutable foundation, Franklin reared his political system. Many other philosophers have developed more original and more perfect conceptions of the political organism. Few of them, however, have exerted a more wholesome influence upon the development of political thought than did Franklin, or have equaled his rare genius for transmuting abstract doctrines of theory into living realities of human government. The political theories of Benjamin Franklin have endured and will continue to endure; for his long life of public service has left them written large in the imperishable annals of the nation.

Bibliography

Manuscript Sources—
The Franklin Papers in William S. Mason private library, Evanston, Ill. American Philosophical Society, Philadelphia, Pa. Pennsylvania Historical Society, Philadelphia, Pa. University of Pennsylvania Library, Philadelphia, Pa.

Bibliographies—
Ford, P. L., *A List of Books Written by or Relating to Benjamin Franklin.* (Brooklyn, 1889.)
Hildeburn, C. S. R., *A Century of Printing; the Issues of the Press in Pennsylvania.* (Philadelphia, 1885-1886.)

Collections of Sources—
American Archives, 5th Series, Vol. II, Ed. by P. Force. (Washington, 1851.)
Collections of the Massachusetts Historical Society, 5th Series, Vol. IX (Boston, 1885.)
The Complete Works of Benjamin Franklin. 10 vols. Ed. by J. Bigelow. (New York, 1888.)
The Correspondence of William Shirley. Ed. by C. H. Lincoln. 2 vols. (New York, 1912.)
Documents Relative to the Colonial History of the State of New York. Vols. IV, VI. Ed. by E. B. O'Callaghan. (Albany, 1855.)
Facsimiles of Manuscripts in European Archives Relating to America, 1773-1783. Ed. by B. F. Stevens. 25 vols. (London, 1889-1898.)
The Federal and State Constitutions and Other Organic Laws of the United States. 2 vols. Ed. by B. P. Poore. (Washington, 1877.)
History of the Celebration of the One Hundredth Anniversary of the Promulgation of the Constitution of the United States. Vol. II. Ed. by H. L. Carson. (Philadelphia, 1889.)

Journals of the Continental Congress. Vols. II, III, IV, V,
    VI, XIX.   Ed. by W. C. Ford.   (Washington, 1905.)
Letters and Papers of Cadwallader Colden.   Vol. IV.   In the
    Collections of the New York Historical Society.   (New
    York, 1920.)
Letters of Members of the Continental Congress.   Vols. I,
    II.   Ed. by E. C. Burnett.   (Washington, 1921.)
The London Chronicle, 1767.
Memoir of the Life of Josiah Quincy, Jr.   Ed. by J. Quincy.
    (Boston, 1825.)
The Parliamentary History of England.   Vols. XVI, XVII,
    XVIII.   Ed. by T. C. Hansard.   (London, 1813.)
Principles and Acts of the Revolution in America.   Ed. by
    H. Niles.   (Baltimore, 1822.)
Records of the Colony of Rhode Island.   Vol. VI.   (Provi-
    dence, 1861.)
The Records of the Federal Convention of 1787.   3 vols.
    Ed. by M. Farrand.   (New Haven, 1911.)
*Treaties, Conventions, International Acts, Protocols and
    Agreements between the United States of America and
    Other Powers.*   Vol. II.   Ed. by W. M. Malloy.
    (Washington, 1910.)
The Works of Benjamin Franklin.   10 vols.   Ed. by J.
    Sparks.   (Chicago, 1882.)
The Works of John Adams.   10 vols.   Ed. by C. F. Adams.
    (Boston, 1866.)
The Works of Thomas Jefferson.   Ed. by P. L. Ford.   10
    vols. in 1892 ed., 12 vols. in 1905 ed.   (New York.)
The Writings of Benjamin Franklin.   10 vols.   Ed. by A.
    H. Smyth.   (New York, 1907.)
The Writings of James Madison.   9 vols.   Ed. by G. Hunt.
    (New York, 1908.)

Treatises on Government, Contemporary Pamphlets, etc.—
    Bland, R., *An Inquiry into the Rights of the British
        Colonies.*   (Williamsburg, 1766.)
    Coxe, D., *A Description of the English Province of Caro-
        lana.*   (London, 1722.)
    Dickinson, J., *Letters from a Farmer in Pennsylvania to the
        Inhabitants of Great Britain.*   (Boston, 1768.)

Bibliography 99

Gargaz, P. A., *A Project of Universal and Perpetual Peace Written by Pierre-André Gargaz, a former Galley Slave, and printed by Benjamin Franklin at Passy in the Year 1782.* Ed. by G. S. Eddy. (New York, 1922.)

Hamilton, A., etc., *The Federalist.* (New York, 1898.)

Harrington, J., *The Oceana and Other Works.* (London, 1747.)

Hobbes, T., *Leviathan.* (Cambridge, 1904.)

Kennedy, A., *The Importance of Gaining and Preserving the Friendship of the Indians to the British Interest Considered.* (London, 1752.)

Knox, W., *The Claim of the Colonies to an Exemption from Internal Taxes Imposed by Authority of Parliament Examined.* (London, 1765.)

Locke, J., Two Treatises of Government. In *Works of John Locke,* Vol. IV. (London, 1824.)

Milton, J., Areopagitica, Tenure of Kings and Magistrates In *Works of John Milton,* Vol. IV. (London, 1851.)

Montesquieu, Baron de, *The Spirit of Laws.* 2 vols. (London, 1878.)

Otis, J., *A Vindication of the British Colonies.* (London, 1769.)

Ramsay, A., *Thoughts on the Origin and Nature of Government.* (London, 1769.) Franklin's copy with his marginal notes now in Library of Congress.

Rousseau, J. J., *The Social Contract.* (London, 1895.)

———, *A Lasting Peace through the Federation of Europe.* (London, 1917.)

Smith, A., *An Inquiry into the Nature and Causes of the Wealth of Nations.* 2 vols. (London, 1904.)

Wheelock, M., *Reflections Moral and Political on Great Britain and her Colonies.* (London, 1777.) Franklin's copy with his marginal notes now in the Library of Congress.

———, *Observations on the Present Government of Pennsylvania.* (Philadelphia, 1777.)

———, *Good Humour or A Way with the Colonies.* (London, 1766.) Franklin's copy with his marginal notes now in the Pennsylvania Historical Society.

Secondary Works—

Adams, R. G., *The Political Ideas of the American Revolution.* (Durham, 1922.)

Becker, C., *The Declaration of Independence.* (New York, 1922.)

Beer, G. L., *British Colonial Policy, 1754-1765.* (New York, 1907.)

Dunning, W. A., *A History of Political Theories from Luther to Montesquieu.* (New York, 1905.)

Dunning, W. A., *A History of Political Theories from Rousseau to Spencer.* (New York, 1920.)

Egerton, H. E., *A Short History of British Colonial Policy.* (London, 1897.)

Fitzpatrick, J. C., *The Spirit of the Revolution.* (New York, 1924.)

Hale, E. E., *Franklin in France.* (Boston, 1887.)

Hazelton, J. H., *The Declaration of Independence: Its History.* (New York, 1906.)

Konkle, B. A., *George Bryan and the Constitution of Pennsylvania, 1731-1791.* (Philadelphia, 1922.)

Merriam, C. E., *A History of American Political Theories.* (New York, 1913.)

Parkman, F., *Montcalm and Wolfe.* 2 vols. (Boston, 1898.)

Russell-Smith, H. F., *Harrington and his Oceana.* (Cambridge, 1914.)

Periodicals—

"The Antecedents of the Declaration of Independence," by J. Sullivan. *Report of the American Historical Association, 1902,* Vol. I, pp. 67-81.

"Benjamin Franklin's Plans for a Colonial Union, 1750-1775," by L. K. Mathews. *American Political Science Review,* Vol. VIII, 393-412.

"Dr. Benjamin Franklin's Library," by G. S. Eddy. *Proceedings of the American Antiquarian Society,* Vol. XXXIV, 206-226.

"Excerpts from the Papers of Doctor Benjamin Rush," *Pennsylvania Magazine of History and Biography,* Vol. XXIX, pp. 15-30.

Bibliography

"Franklin and the Physiocrats," by F. W. Garrison. *The Freeman*, October 24, 1923.

"Franklin's Articles of Confederation," by W. C. Ford. *The Nation*, Vol. XLVIII, 261-263.

"Harrington and his Influence upon American Political Institutions and American Thought," by T. W. Dwight. *Political Science Quarterly*, Vol. II, pp. 1-44.

"A Missing Chapter of Franco-American History," by D. J. Hill. *American Historical Review*, Vol. XXI, pp. 709-719.

"Party Struggles over the First Pennsylvania Constitution," by S. B. Harding. *Report of the American Historical Association*, 1894, pp. 371-402.

"Rousseau in Philadelphia." *Magazine of American History*, Vol. XII, pp. 46-55.